PHARAOHS, VILLAINS AND THIEVES

ANITA GANERI

An imprint of HarperCollins*Publishers*

Pharaohs, Villains and Thieves accompanies the television series *Ancient Egyptians* created by Wall to Wall for Channel Four, TLC ® and Granada International in association with Canal+, Norddeutscher Rundfunk/Germany, RAI – Radiotelevisione Italiana, Seven Network Australia and Warner Home Video Inc., A Warner Bros. Entertainment Company.

First published in Great Britain by HarperCollins*Publishers* Ltd in 2003
Text copyright © 2003 HarperCollins*Publishers* Ltd,
77-85 Fulham Palace Road, Hammersmith, London W6 8JB
Photographs by Giles Keyte © Wall to Wall (Egypt) Ltd 2002

wall to wall

The Wall to Wall website address is: www.walltowall.co.uk

The HarperCollins website address is: www.harpercollins.co.uk

1 3 5 7 9 10 8 6 4 2
ISBN 0-00-715377-5

Designer: Elorine Grant
Cover Designer: James Annal
Illustrator: Tim Stevens
Editor: Terry Vittachi
Consultant: Dr Ian Shaw

Printed and bound in Great Britain by Clays Ltd, St Ives plc

CONTENTS

INTRODUCTION

Welcome to ancient Egypt!

Thousands of years ago, the splendid civilisation of ancient Egypt flourished along the banks of the River Nile. It was ruled by powerful pharaohs who built great temples, tombs and towns. Most ordinary Egyptians were farmers. They grew crops in fields made fertile by the river's annual flood. But who were the ancient Egyptians and what were their lives really like?

The four stories in this book are all based on actual written records about real Egyptians who lived centuries ago. Our evidence for The Twins, for example, comes from a collection of ancient texts found inside a huge pot. It had lain hidden for more than two thousand years. The records give us a rare glimpse into a fascinating world. Through the eyes of the characters, we can experience what life was like for pharaohs and ordinary soldiers, aristocrats and priests, great officials and lowly tomb robbers, lawyers, humble farmers and interpreters of dreams alike. In addition, the stories are spread over time. Each one opens a window into a different and exciting period of Egyptian history, from the heights of the New Kingdom to Egypt under Greek rule. This is history - but not as you've seen it before!

First published in Great Britain by HarperCollins*Publishers* Ltd in 2003 to accompany the Channel Four television series *Ancient Egyptians*.

CHAPTER ONE

THE BATTLE OF MEGIDDO

Main characters in the story:

Ahmose (*Ark-mows-ay*) – *soldier in Egyptian army*

Tuthmosis III (*Tut-mow-sis*) – *Pharaoh of Egypt*

Nakht (*Nack-t*) – *a Nubian soldier in Tuthmosis's army*

Djehuty (*Juh-hoot-ee*) – *a general in Tuthmosis's army*

Yamunedj (*Yam-un-edge*) – *a general in Tuthmosis's army*

Nefer (*Neff-ur*) – *Ahmose's girlfriend*

Tjeneni (*Tcher-nen-ee*) – *royal scribe on Tuthmosis III's campaigns*

The Prince of Kadesh – *(a city in Syria)*

INTRODUCTION

ON 15 MAY 1458 BC, dawn was beginning to break over the city of Megiddo in Palestine (modern-day Israel). But this was to be no ordinary day. On the great plain outside the city walls, the Prince of Kadesh made a last inspection of his lines. Above them, from his vantage point on the hillside, Pharaoh Tuthmosis III stood in his war chariot at the head of the Egyptian army. In time-honoured fashion, the Pharaoh was dressed for battle in a golden headdress, with a bow in his hand and a quiver of arrows over his shoulder. As he surveyed the scene below, he looked confident and assured. This was his moment of destiny when he could prove himself as a mighty ruler. The time had come. With a loud blast, the trumpets sounded and the soldiers rattled their weapons on their shields. This was the signal they'd been waiting for – let the battle begin.

Among the ranks of the Egyptians stood a young soldier called Ahmose, who was nervously fingering a good-luck pendant which hung on a leather string around his neck. Several months before, he and thousands of young men like him had been called up from the villages of Egypt to serve in the army. They went from being farmers to being the soldiers of a new Pharaoh. A young scribe, Tjeneni, was also there to record the day's events. Later, the words of his battle report were carved in hieroglyphs on the walls of the great Temple of Karnak in Thebes – the oldest detailed account of a battle ever recorded. It told the story of a turning point in Egyptian history when a young, untried Pharaoh emerged as one of the greatest of all warrior-kings.

PART ONE

Harvest time

IN THE HUNDREDS OF VILLAGES along the banks of the River Nile, life had not changed for centuries. Nine-tenths of Egyptians were peasants working along the banks of the Nile. Each year, in July, the river flooded, depositing a layer of mud and silt on the farmers' fields and creating a rich, black soil which was ideal for growing crops. Now, like generations of farmers before them, Ahmose and his family were busy with the year's harvest. But Ahmose also had other things on his mind. He had fallen in love with a girl called Nefer. And he was watching her every movement as she helped the other women collect up bundles of palm fronds.

With the harvest gathered in, the farming year drew to a close. Soon the fields would be covered with flood water, and work would come to a halt. Usually, there was little for farmers to do for a few months but wait for the waters to fall back again. But for many young Egyptian men like Ahmose, this year would be different.

GIFT OF THE NILE

The River Nile was vital for all Egyptian life. It provided water for drinking and irrigation and, when it flooded, it created fertile soil for farming in land that would otherwise have been bone-dry desert. In fact, the river was so important that the Egyptians called their country 'the gift of the Nile'. The farmer's year was based around the yearly flood, or inundation...

JULY – NOVEMBER
The inundation
The fields were covered with water so work stopped. Some farmers were called up to work on royal building sites or to join the army.

NOVEMBER – MARCH
The growing season
As the waters went down, the farmers ploughed their fields and sowed their seeds. Then they watered and weeded their crops.

MARCH – JULY
The harvest
The whole village joined in. Before the harvest was gathered, an official calculated how much grain the farmer had to give to the Pharaoh in taxes.

Rulers and rebellions

MEANWHILE, IN HIS SUMPTUOUS ROYAL APPARTMENTS at Thebes, Tuthmosis III was in his robing room, being dressed by his servant in the Pharaoh's finery. In ancient Egypt, the Pharaoh was thought to be a divine being, descended from the god Amun-Re. His presence was sacred and his rule was law. For over twenty years, Egypt had been ruled by Queen Hatshepsut. Now she was dead and power had been handed over to Tuthmosis, her young step-son. The new Pharaoh was in his mid-twenties, handsome, athletic and ambitious. In fact, he had held the title of Pharaoh since the death of his father when he was a young boy. But, as the son of one of the old King's minor wives, he had never been allowed to rule. Instead, power had been seized by his father's Chief Wife, Hatshepsut, leaving Tuthmosis Pharaoh in name only. Now it was his turn to rule alone. But what sort of leader would the dashing young prince prove to be?

The people of Egypt did not have to wait long for Tuthmosis to make his mark. To the north, in Palestine, local rulers had begun a revolt against Egyptian power. For two generations Egypt had ruled Palestine and Syria, demanding high taxes in gold and silver to be paid to the Pharaoh in return for peace. During Hatshepsut's reign, however, the Egyptians' hold on the region had gradually grown weaker. Now, with a new Pharaoh on the throne, the Prince of Kadesh seized his chance. Under his leadership, a full-scale rebellion had begun, and even now the Prince and his allies were moving their forces towards Egypt's northern border.

HATSHEPSUT

Hatshepsut began her rule (1473-1458BC) as regent for her stepson, Tuthmosis III, but she later seized the throne for herself. Female Pharaohs were very rare in Egypt so Hatshepsut had herself crowned 'king'. Inscriptions referred to her as 'His Majesty', and statues showed her dressed in the traditional clothes of a male Pharaoh, complete with a false beard. Her reign is best remembered for her trading missions and amazing buildings. In about 1480BC, she sent an expedition to the land of Punt to bring back precious goods, such as myrrh, incense, ebony and ivory. Her most famous building was her mortuary temple in Thebes, Deir el-Bahari. Inside, its walls were decorated with paintings of events in Hatshepsut's life.

It was the Pharaoh's duty to protect his kingdom and his people from attack, so for Tuthmosis the rebellion was an opportunity to prove himself as Pharaoh. In the royal palace, he gathered his generals around him and began to make plans to put the rebel forces down.

Heading to war

FOR SUCH A MAJOR CAMPAIGN, the Pharaoh needed to boost the numbers of soldiers in his army. His officials kept records of every able-bodied man who could be released from working on the land to work for the Pharaoh instead. Most years, this meant thousands of villagers being put to work in quarries, or building temples, tombs and canals. But the same records were also used to draft extra men into the army.

So, when Ahmose saw the scribe and soldiers marching into his village, he knew what was coming and was filled with dread. What he hadn't expected was that the scribe would pick his younger brother instead of him. Before Nefer could stop him, he stepped forward to protest.

"Take me instead of my brother," he begged. "He is too young to go to war. Let him stay here."

A short while later, it was Ahmose who left his house, carrying his few possessions – a goatskin water bottle, a spare loincloth, his shaving kit and some bread and dried fish. A soldier guarded the doorway to make sure he didn't make a run for it. Nefer knew that it might be years before she saw Ahmose again, even if he made it back alive. Fighting back the tears, she took a pendant from around her neck and put it around his for good luck. Then, with one last glance at his home, his family and Nefer – everything he loved most in the world – Ahmose was led away.

PART TWO

Tactics for war

THE FORTRESS CITY OF MEGIDDO sat at the crossroads of the great trading routes of the ancient Middle East. Whoever ruled Megiddo could control the whole surrounding region. After Queen Hatshepsut's death, the Prince of Kadesh and his allies had seized the city. From here, the rebel army planned to move its forces south towards the Egyptian border. But, as the leaders met to discuss their battle tactics, an Egyptian spy was hiding in the shadows, listening to every word they said.

Meanwhile, Pharaoh Tuthmosis moved his war headquarters from Thebes to the fortress of Tjaru in the north east. Travelling with the Pharaoh and his army was the young scribe, Tjeneni, whose job was to write the official report of the coming campaign. This is how his diary began: *"Year 22, fourth month of the second season, on the twenty-fifth day his Majesty was in Tjaru on the first victorious expedition to extend the boundaries of Egypt by force... Now, at that time, it happened that the Asiatic tribes, the people who were in Sharuhen, and from Yeraza to the marshes of the Earth, had begun to revolt against his Majesty..."*

As Tjeneni continued writing, Tuthmosis and three of his trusty generals were questioning the Egyptian spy...

Life of a soldier

FOR THE NEXT FEW MONTHS, Tjaru was also to be Ahmose's new home. Throughout the winter of 1458BC, thousands of recruits like Ahmose arrived at Tjaru. The fortress was the major garrison on the north-east border, where the Pharaoh was gathering ten thousand men. Ahmose and his

SCRIBES AND WRITING

Scribes like Tjeneni were highly respected in ancient Egypt. Egyptian writing used signs, called hieroglyphs, which stood for sounds and objects. These were extremely complicated and most ordinary Egyptians could not understand them. Scribes spent years at special schools, learning to read and write. Their writing skills brought them status and power. Scribes could get good jobs in temples or in the Pharaoh's service. Tjeneni was employed by Tuthmosis III to keep a daily diary of the Megiddo campaign. He went on to become a general in his own right and served Tuthmosis for 31 years. When Tjeneni died, he was granted a tomb among those of the nobles of Thebes – a very great honour indeed.

companions were led into the fortress by two soldiers. Few of them had ever been far from their villages before and it felt a very long way from home. As they were marched through the enclosure, full of men, donkeys and noise, Ahmose stared up at the imposing walls and wished he were back home again.

The new recruits were ordered to line up in front of a scribe who wrote down their names. In case any of them decided to make a break for it, a soldier stood ready with a stick. Then the men queued up for food. Each recruit had a supply of tokens to pay for his daily ration of food. Ahmose handed a token over and was given porridge, bread and beer. But as he turned round, he collided with a burly Nubian soldier, and dropped his bread on the ground. With a mumbled apology, Ahmose picked up his bread, brushed off the dirt and got out of the Nubian's way, fast. He didn't want any trouble. Meanwhile, the Nubian, whose name was Nakht, collected his rations and went to sit with his fellow countrymen. For not all of the soldiers in the Pharaoh's army were Egyptians. Archers, infantry and scouts were also drawn from the lands to the south of Egypt, such as Nubia

As Ahmose quickly found out, the months spent at Tjaru were all about learning to fight. His training in hand-to-hand combat began almost immediately. As a foot soldier, he would be in the thick of the action, once the chariots had broken through the enemy lines. And he'd need to be fearless and fast on his feet. His life would depend on it. Armed with an axe or a spear, his only protection against his enemy's weapons would be a wood and leather shield. But it was not just the ordinary soldiers who needed to perfect their battle skills. Outside the fortress, the Pharaoh and his generals were taking part in archery practice. From an early age, Tuthmosis had been trained in the art of warfare. The Pharaohs of Egypt were supposed to be the greatest warriors of their day. As his arrow hit the target, Tuthmosis smiled triumphantly. But whether he would live up to his reputation was yet to be seen.

EGYPTIAN ARMY

During the New Kingdom (1552-1069BC), warrior-pharaohs like Tuthmosis needed huge armies to help them expand their empire. The Pharaoh was Commander-in-Chief and often planned and led campaigns himself. The army was made up of divisions of 5,000 men (4,000 foot soldiers and 1,000 charioteers) and each division was named after a god. At Megiddo, there were thought to be two divisions (10,000 men). The chariots fought in the front line. Behind them were the experienced soldiers. Less experienced recruits brought up the rear. Weapons included spears, axes and daggers made from bronze and wood, bows made from wood or horn, and arrows tipped with ivory. Most soldiers had wood and leather shields. Only the highest-ranking officers could afford bronze and leather armour.

Wrestling match

LATER THAT EVENING, with training over for the day, Ahmose sat in the crowd to watch a bout of wrestling between Nakht the Nubian and one of the Egyptian soldiers. Wrestling was the Egyptians' favourite sport and the Nubians were reckoned to be the best wrestlers of all. And so it seemed. With barely any effort, Nakht threw the other man to the ground and was declared the winner. But who would be his next opponent? Menacingly, Nakht paced up and down in front of the crowd and stopped... in front of Ahmose. In comparison with the huge Nubian, Ahmose looked horribly puny, and petrified. He had good reason to be scared. For Egyptian wrestling could be bloody and brutal, and bouts sometimes went on until one of the contestants was unconscious. As Nakht lunged towards him, Ahmose just managed to duck out of the way but then took a tumble. No sooner had he found his feet than Nakht knocked him down again. And again. Then an astonishing thing happened. Summoning all his strength and anger, Ahmose came out fighting for his life... and pinned Nakht to the ground. The stunned crowd fell silent. How would the champion react to this shocking defeat? Slowly, Nakht began to pick himself up off the floor and dust himself down. Ahmose held out his hand to help him up. Without a word, Nakht took Ahmose's hand and... lifted an amazed Ahmose up on to his shoulders.

But the games were about to come to an end...

PART THREE

On the march

THE FOLLOWING SPRING, the army of Tuthmosis III left the fortress of Tjaru and began its long, dusty march through the desert into Palestine. This is how Tjeneni, the scribe, described their departure:

"Year 23, first month of the third season. On the fifth day, we left this place in might, in power and in triumph to overthrow that wretched foe, to extend the boundaries of Egypt, just as his father Amun-Re had commanded."

At the head of the huge army rode the Pharaoh in his chariot, surrounded by his most trusted followers. For these generals, being close to the Pharaoh meant positions of power and the promise of great riches. But life was very different for ordinary soldiers like Ahmose. As he and his thousands of companions marched behind, their feet kicked up clouds of choking dust so that they could barely see or breathe. No matter how fit and strong they were, many men were forced to drop out of the ranks.

Exhausted, Ahmose and some of his fellow soldiers stopped for a well-earned rest. They were soon joined by Nakht the Nubian, who tried to raise his friend's flagging spirits.

"You've got to keep going," Nakht told him. "Otherwise, who will beat me at wrestling?"

But Ahmose was too weary to reply. Next to him, a soldier rubbed oil on his blistered feet and wrapped them in two ragged pieces of cloth. Then he trudged grimly on. This is how another scribe described a soldier's life in a letter warning his son not to join the army:

"He is called up for Syria. He may not rest. There are not clothes, not sandals… He drinks water every three days: it smells foul and tastes of salt. His body is ravaged by illness… His body is weak, his legs fail him… he is worn out from marching."

Soldiers were just as likely to die from disease as from any actual fighting. But death itself was not the most frightening thing of all for an Egyptian soldier. It was the thought of dying away from home that terrified them. Only if they were buried inside Egypt's borders would they stand a chance of reaching a better life in the Next World. Otherwise, they faced a fate worse than death, with their souls being cast into chaos. Running away was not an option. Every soldier knew that, even if he escaped, his family, including his wife and children, would be forced to do hard labour for life. For Ahmose, there was nothing to do but to accept his fate.

Council of war

TWO MONTHS AFTER LEAVING TJARU, an exhausted and foot-sore army reached the oasis of Yehem in Palestine. The Egyptians were now just fifty kilometres south of the rebel stronghold at Megiddo.

Standing outside his tent, Tuthmosis looked out over the vast army camp sprawled out across the valley below. It was an anxious time for the Pharaoh as he contemplated what lay ahead. But his thoughts were soon disturbed by the arrival of his generals. For, here at Yehem, the young Pharaoh had called a council of war. Tuthmosis ushered them into his tent. Tjeneni, the scribe, was close behind, as always. The problem to be debated was this: which way should they advance on Megiddo?

One of the generals, Yamunedj, pulled back the reed mat

covering the floor and drew a map in the sand with his spear. There were three routes open to them, Yamunedj explained:

"Two routes run to the north and south. They are the safest but also the longest. The third way is through the Aruna Pass. This is the shortest and quickest route, but it's also the most dangerous. The valley's so narrow that the men will only be able to travel in single file, making them easy targets to be ambushed."

Yamunedj looked anxiously at the Pharaoh, who was pacing up and down, deep in thought. What would he decide to do? Tuthmosis picked up a spear and traced a line on the map... right along the third and riskiest route. To his generals' dismay, he had decided to take a gamble and march to Megiddo through the perilous Aruna Pass.

Another general, Djehuty, broke the stunned silence, "But your Majesty, with due respect, our spies tell us that if we go this way, our enemy will be waiting for us. They will pick off our men one by one as they leave the Pass. I beg you, please think again."

But Tuthmosis would not be swayed. Young and inexperienced though he was, he was also determined to prove his worth once and for all.

"My mind is made up," he replied. "I will take the road to Aruna. Because it's so dangerous our enemies won't expect us to come this way. We will catch them off guard and buy ourselves time. If any of you want to follow the other routes, then go. Those who wish can follow me. If I take another route, what will the Prince of Kadesh think? That the Pharaoh of Egypt is afraid of him? That is what he will say."

"We will follow you, your Majesty," Djehuty said, quietly.

"Then, tell the army that I myself will lead them through the pass," added Tuthmosis.

To give his generals and his army the confidence to face the coming battle, the daring Pharaoh decided to lead the way through the Aruna Pass, placing himself in just as much danger as his men.

Through the Pass

NEXT DAY, AT DAYBREAK, Pharaoh Tuthmosis III led his army into the Aruna Pass. As always, Tjeneni was there, ready to record the Pharaoh's every move.

"He went forth at the head of his army himself, showing the way by his own footsteps; horse behind horse, his majesty at the head of his army."

In single file, the soldiers followed him, snaking their way through the pass. On either side sheer rock cliffs loomed menacingly above their heads. Well aware of the danger, Yamunedj and Djehuty kept looking up as if expecting to see enemy archers at any minute. It was a twelve hour march through the Pass and all the way the men were open to ambush from above. They were quiet and jumpy, and the tension was almost unbearable. Especially when a loose stone suddenly broke free and bounced noisily down the rockface…

At the head of his men, Tuthmosis climbed on, grim-faced and determined. Neither he nor his generals spotted the figure of a lone enemy spy, silhouetted against the sky. Silently, the spy surveyed the army, then disappeared from view. Back in the Prince of Kadesh's tent in Taanach, the spy relayed his news. At once, a look of panic spread across the Prince's face. For, against all the odds, the Pharaoh's gamble had paid off. The Prince of Kadesh and his forces had been waiting for them on the *southern* route, sure that the Egyptians would avoid the Pass at all costs. There was barely time for Kadesh to move camp and join his allies at Megiddo.

Meanwhile, the Egyptians found their road to Megiddo open and clear.

The eve of battle

BY THE TIME THE EGYPTIANS REACHED MEGIDDO, it was too late in the day for the fighting to start. Tuthmosis gave the order for his men to set up camp. Then he rode out in his chariot on to the plain, accompanied by his generals. On the hill in front of them stood the fortress-city of Megiddo. Tuthmosis turned to Yamunedj.

"All the princes of the northern countries are trapped inside the city. Capturing Megiddo will be like capturing a thousand towns."

Later, in his tent, Tuthmosis made an offering of bread, milk and meat to Amun-Re, king of the gods, with the following prayer:

"You are Amun-Re, Lord of Thebes, who rescues those who are in need. For you are merciful. When I appeal to you, you come from afar."

Then the Pharaoh sent a command to the army,

"Arm yourselves! Prepare your weapons! For we shall advance to fight the enemy in the morning."

In the crowded army camp, Ahmose sat quietly, fingering his pendant and thinking over the Pharaoh's words. Tomorrow he would fight his first battle. But would he make it back alive?

PART FOUR

Oil and offerings

IT WAS DAWN ON THE DAY OF BATTLE. Over the centuries, the great walled city of Megiddo had been a horribly unlucky place, jealously fought over in battle after battle. Now in the spring of 1458BC, Megiddo was preparing to defend itself against the army of Pharaoh Tuthmosis III.

On the Plain of Megiddo, the Pharaoh stood ready in his royal chariot at the head of his vast army. Tjeneni, the scribe, set the scene:

"Year 23, first month of the third season, on the twenty-first day, the day of the feast of the new moon. Early in the morning command was given to the entire army to move. His majesty rode out in a chariot, dressed in his weapons of war, like Horus, the Smiter, lord of power; like Montu of Thebes, god of battle; while his father, Amun-Re, gave strength to his army."

But could the Pharaoh live up to Tjeneni's fine words? To his left and right, across the hillsides, were ranged the Egyptian foot soldiers and archers, among them Ahmose and Nakht, and in the centre were the chariots, and Tuthmosis himself. Just before battle began, officers passed down the lines of men, anointing them with scented oil for protection. Then, as the Prince of Kadesh and four enemy chiefs emerged from the city gates, Tuthmosis made the sign they'd been waiting for. The trumpets sounded. The men rattled their weapons against the shields. And the Battle of Megiddo began...

The Battle of Megiddo

WITH PHARAOH TUTHMOSIS AT THEIR HEAD, the Egyptian chariots led the charge against the enemy. In each chariot stood a driver and an officer in armour, bow at the ready. As they approached the enemy front lines, the archers let fly a shower of arrows. Their aim was to cause chaos and break the lines up so that the foot soldiers could move in. Soon, Ahmose and Nakht were in the thick of battle, fighting for their lives. And still the Pharaoh led the attack. Tjeneni reported what happened next:

"And when the enemy soldiers saw his majesty, they fled to Megiddo in fear, abandoning their horses and their chariots."

Driven back by the chariot charge, the Prince of Kadesh and many of his soldiers ran towards the city's wooden gates. Once inside, they would be safe. But, to their horror, the gates of the city were already shut and the Prince was trapped. But all was not lost. In the confusion that followed, the people of the city threw ropes made of clothing over the battlements and managed to haul the Prince and many of his soldiers up and over the walls to safety. As the men scrambled desperately up the ropes, the Egyptians hurled axes at them. Sometimes a rope snapped in two, sending the soldiers plummeting into the hands of the Egyptians. Beneath the walls, the bloody battle still raged. Grimly, Ahmose and Nakht fought their way through the chaos.

The Egyptians had victory in their grasp, but instead of chasing after the rebels and storming the city, the soldiers' thoughts turned to looting. Ahmose and Nakht picked their way carefully through the enemy bodies stretched out on the ground. All around them, Egyptian soldiers were stealing weapons, armour and jewellery from the dead and wounded. After a moment's hesitation, Ahmose and Nakht joined in. After all, this was the only reward an ordinary foot soldier would get. Meanwhile, the remaining rebel soldiers were safely inside the city. If only the Egyptians had not been so busy plundering, they could have captured Megiddo there and then.

Ahmose bent down to pick up a valuable weapon. He could use it, or sell it later on. At least, that was the plan. Just at that moment, a wounded enemy soldier picked up his axe and, with the last of his strength, struck Ahmose with a brutal blow to the head. His face twisted with pain and streaming with blood, Ahmose slumped to the ground.

A Pharaoh's fury

LATER THAT NIGHT, Tuthmosis walked across the battlefield, dusty and bloody from the day's fighting. All around the ground was strewn with bodies, some still clinging on to life.

And all around Egyptian soldiers wandered about, looting anything of value. Some were even pulling used arrows out of corpses. Angrily, Tuthmosis surveyed the scene. For this was not the victorious outcome the young Pharaoh had been banking on.

When he returned to his tent, his generals were waiting nervously. With great ceremony, Djehuty's servant placed a large basket down by the Pharaoh's feet. But Tuthmosis barely gave it a second glance. He was furious that they had failed to capture Megiddo.

"Every one of the enemy princes is inside the city," he snarled at the shame-faced generals. "If you'd captured the city while you had the chance, our work would be done. But now, instead of glory, we'll be locked into a lengthy siege."

Tuthmosis looked down at the basket in front of him and gave it a hefty kick. It fell on its side and out of it spilled over seventy severed hands – the hands of the enemy dead, offered to the Pharaoh in return for gold – which splattered the generals in blood. Then Tuthmosis stormed out of his tent.

A soldier's death

OVER IN THE SOLDIERS' CAMP, the army surgeon was busy treating the men wounded in battle. In those days, most soldiers died after the fighting was over, from shock, loss of blood and infection. Egyptian doctors were highly skilled. In fact, many of their skills were learned on the battlefield, and their manuals listed hundreds of remedies. The surgeon now moved slowly down the line of injured men. Some wounds were simple to treat. To stop a wound from bleeding, the surgeon placed a red-hot knife blade on it. Honey was an excellent dressing for burns and helped to keep wounds clean. But not every wounded soldier could be helped so easily. Some injuries were so serious that there was very little the surgeon could do...

Nakht walked anxiously among the injured soldiers, looking for Ahmose. Eventually he found his friend, but Ahmose was a pitiful sight. His upper body had been tied to a post to stop him from moving. The gaping wound on his head was being cleaned by a doctor. But the wound was still bleeding and Nakht knew that Ahmose was in a very bad way. Head wounds were the most common battle injury in Egyptian times. The treatment was to put a piece of fresh meat on the wound to stop it bleeding, and to keep the patient still. But it didn't always work. As Nakht knelt down beside him, Ahmose opened his eyes.

"You've been a good friend," Ahmose whispered. "And I want you to take this."

He pressed something into Nakht's hand. It was his precious good-luck pendant, given to him by Nefer so many months ago. Tears streamed down Nakht's face.

"I will take good care of it, my friend," he said.

Then Ahmose died.

Siege and surrender

FOR SEVEN LONG MONTHS, the Egyptians laid seige to Megiddo. They built a moat and a wooden palisade around the city – no one could leave. Now the people inside the city were running desperately short. Soon they would starve to death. Faced with this bleak future, the enemy leaders, including the Prince of Kadesh, had no choice but to surrender.

One winter's day, the great gates of Megiddo creaked open and a procession of children walked out of the city. They looked frightened, hungry and dirty, and stood blinking in the bright sunlight. In their arms they carried gifts of gold, jewels and weapons for the Egyptian Pharaoh. In handing their children over, the rebels showed that they accepted Egyptian rule. According to custom, these children would be taken hostage and brought up as Egyptians, the adopted children of the Pharaoh. For Tuthmosis, this was a great victory. In putting down the rebellion and bringing Palestine and Syria back under Egyptian rule, he had proved himself to be a great warrior and earned his place in history.

Triumph and tears

TUTHMOSIS'S TRIUMPHANT RETURN TO THEBES was marked by a fabulous feast which lasted for five days. Then it was time for the Pharaoh to face his people. Sumptuously dressed, with the red and white crown of Egypt on his head, and surrounded by his generals and courtiers, Tuthmosis III slowly climbed the steps to the Window of Appearances. From the window, the Pharaoh threw down gold necklaces, bracelets and other gifts to his most trusted soldiers. A huge crowd gathered in the courtyard to see their Pharaoh in all his finery. They watched as the enemy chiefs bowed down before their new ruler and handed over gifts as a sign of their surrender. The scribe, Tjeneni, wrote grandly:

"Behold, the chiefs of this country came to render their portions, to do obeisance to the fame of his majesty, to crave

TUTHMOSIS III

Tuthmosis III (ruled from 1479-1425BC) was one of Egypt's greatest warrior-pharaohs. After Hatshepsut's death, Tuthmosis immediately formed an army and set off to restore Egypt's empire to its former glory. The Battle of Megiddo was the most famous of his career, and established his reputation as a brilliant leader and soldier. Over the next 20 years he fought and won another 17 campaigns in Palestine and Syria and expanded the Egyptian empire to its greatest size. When he died in 1425BC, he was buried in the Valley of the Kings, near Thebes, but his body was later moved to a secret tomb at Deir el-Bahari, to hide it from tomb robbers. The mummy of Tuthmosis III is now on display in the Egyptian Museum in Cairo.

breath for their nostrils, because of the greatness of his power, because of the might of the fame of his majesty the country came to his fame, bearing their gifts of silver, gold, lapis lazuli, malachite, grain and wine…"

But Tjeneni left the last words of his account to the defeated Prince of Kadesh:

"Never again will we do evil against Tuthmosis, may he live for ever, our lord, in our lifetime, for we have witnessed his power. Let him only give breath to us according to his wishes."

Many miles away, in a village by the River Nile, a young woman sat sobbing, her arms wrapped round her knees. In her hand, Nefer held a pendant hung on a leather string. Nakht the Nubian stood next to her. Behind them in the fields, children were playing and farmers were tending their crops. Just another day in ancient Egypt.

THE **BATTLE** OF **MEGIDDO**

On the day of battle, Pharaoh Tuthmosis III, King of Egypt, surveys the lines of his troops from his war chariot.

Among the ranks of Egyptian soldiers is Ahmose, who now advances, still wearing his lucky amulet around hs neck.

Nakht, an expert wrestler, chooses Ahmose as his next opponent. To Nakht's amazement, Ahmose fights furiously and is set to spring a big surprise.

From the ramparts of Megiddo, archers from the rebel army try to defend the city against Egyptian attack.

The standard bearer of the Egyptian army marches in front of the soldiers on their way to war.

TOMB ROBBERS

In the Great Temple of Karnak, officials wait for Amenpanufer's trial to begin.

The tomb robber, Amenpanufer, hides his bundle of stolen goods in a hole in a wall near his home in Thebes.

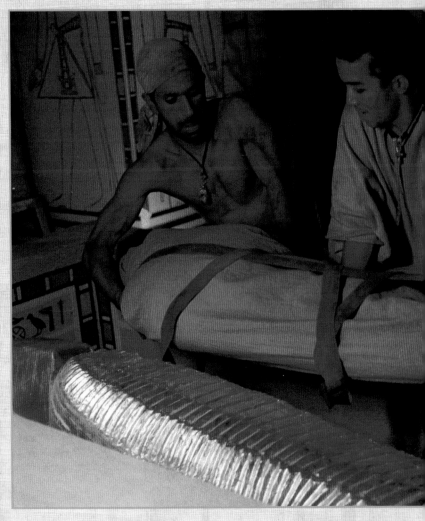

In King Sobekemsaf's tomb, the robbers break into the king's coffin and drag out his mummy. They do not want the mummy itself, but the precious gold and jewellery and other objects hidden in its wrappings.

Amenpanufer hurries down a street in Thebes, clutching his sack of stolen tomb goods.

Murder
in the Temple

Petiese, the Pharaoh's representataive, stands in the courtyard of the Temple of Amun in Teudjoi.

Karem and Ibi run for their lives as they flee through the temple courtyard from the priests who are attacking them.

the TWINS

Taous and Tages in mourning for the sacred bull, dressed in ragged clothes, their hair matted and their faces covered in ash.

The twins with Ptolemaios's brother, Apollonius, on their way to see the temple notary.

The mummified body of the sacred bull is carried through the streets of Memphis on its way to be buried in Saqqara.

The blood of the sacred bull running off the embalming table, where it is being mummified.

CHAPTER TWO

TOMB ROBBERS

Main characters in the story:

Amenpanufer (*Ah-men-pan-oo-fur*) – *quarryman; tomb robber*

Khaemwese (*Car-em-way-zee*) – *Vizier (Prime Minister)*

Paser (*Pay-sa*) – *mayor of East Thebes*

Pawero (*Pa [like pat] -ware-o*) – *mayor of West Thebes*

Pentaweret (*Pent-ah-ware-ette*) – *painter; tomb robber*

Bakwerel (*Back-weral*) – *chief of the Medjay police*

Harshire (*Hah-sheer-ray*) – *chief scribe*

INTRODUCTION

IN THE SIXTEENTH YEAR of the reign of Pharaoh Ramesses IX, on the twenty-second day of the third month of the inundation, the Great Court of Thebes met in the Temple of Karnak. Early in the morning, the High Priest and his officials gathered. Among them were the bitter rivals, Paser, Mayor of East Thebes, and Pawero, Mayor of West Thebes. Next to Pawero sat a sinister-looking man with a livid scar across one cheek and eyebrow. This was Bakwerel, the much-feared chief of the Medjay police.

As they settled in their seats, a door opened and two guards dragged a man before the court, his face bruised and battered. He had been arrested for robbing the tomb of one of Egypt's kings – one of the worst crimes possible. The man, Amenpanufer, knelt before the Vizier, the Pharaoh's representative, who presided over the court, and began his damning confession. Every word was recorded by the court scribe:

"We found the tomb of King Sobekemsaf. It was unlike the tombs we usually robbed. We climbed through a hole in the wall, using candles to give us light. We found furniture, gold and jewellery piled up in the tomb. We shared it out between us and stuffed it into sacks. Then we returned to Thebes..."

As Amenpanufer was speaking, Paser and Pawero exchanged dark looks. For what should have been an open-and-shut case had become a power struggle between the two highest authorities in Thebes. The scribe's record of the trial and the investigation leading up to it has survived for over three thousand years. It tells an extraordinary true story of crime, corruption and lies at the heart of the Egyptian government.

PART ONE

City in crisis

THEBES, THE SACRED CITY OF UPPER EGYPT, was split in two by the River Nile. On the West Bank of Thebes, where the sun set, was the Valley of the Kings where generations of Egypt's Pharaohs were buried in hidden tombs. This was one of the most sacred sites in Egypt. Its mayor, appointed by the Pharaoh, was Pawero, as corrupt and conniving as he was brilliant and charming. As guardian of the royal tombs, this Theban aristocrat held one of the most sensitive jobs in Egypt.

Meanwhile, on the East Bank, the bustling city of Thebes clustered around the vast Temple of Karnak, dedicated to the great god, Amun-Re. The mayor of East Thebes was a nobleman, called Paser, whose family had served the Pharaoh loyally for many years. Unlike his arch-rival Pawero, Paser was in charge of the land of the living. With its temples, shrine and sanctuaries, Thebes was the religious centre of Egypt. But it was no longer the royal capital. Four-and-a-half centuries after the conquests of Tuthmosis III, the Pharaoh's court had moved north. Now in 1111BC, Thebes was a city under strain. A series of bad harvests had made life extremely difficult for its inhabitants. The price of wheat had quadrupled and many ordinary Thebans could not afford enough to eat. It was a time for poor people to find new ways of making ends meet. Among them was a man called Amenpanufer, a labourer in one of the stone quarries across the river in West Thebes. His was a hard life with few prospects, apart from scraping a living.

One day Amenpanufer, a wiry young man with cropped hair and a stubbly beard, was walking through the busy market place, a leather workbag tucked under his arm. The crowd parted to let the Vizier and his entourage pass. With his sumptuous clothes and fancy wig, the Vizier was the most important man in Thebes, and well he knew it. Amenapufer looked at his finery with contempt, then hurried out of the market and home.

Stolen goods

IN CONTRAST TO THE VIZIER'S FINE PALACE, Amenpanufer's home was small and poorly furnished. Inside sat Amenpanufer's wife, nursing a new-born baby. Three young children played around her feet. Amenpanufer went into the main room and opened his leather bag. It was full of small, jewelled objects – a turquoise scarab set in gold, a dazzling necklace inlaid with precious stones... Carefully, he wrapped them in another piece of leather and bound them tightly with a piece of palm fibre. Then he went outside into the courtyard, and hid the bundle in a hole in the wall.

For Amenpanufer was not just a quarryman. He was also a tomb robber. There were rich pickings to be had on the other side of the Nile, in the tombs of wealthy Theban aristocrats. The rich and powerful of ancient Egypt were buried with everything they needed for a luxurious afterlife. But why should the privileged few have it all? Disturbing the tombs was a serious crime, punishable by death and the wrath of the gods. For a poor man like Amenpanufer, though, the rewards were much too tempting to overlook. And he wasn't the only man in Thebes who was not put off by the fear of what the gods might have in store for him.

Later, in a quiet alleyway, Amenpanufer had a secret meeting with another man. In a city like Thebes, anything could be bought and sold. Everything had its price, and Amenpanufer had the most valuable goods of all to sell. They might be illegal, but there were plenty of people interested in buying. Amenpanufer was already well known to the authorities. Four years ago, he had been caught red-handed with goods from the tomb of King Sobekemsaf. But he had managed to bribe an official to get out of trouble. Since then, he had carried on robbing tombs, but he wasn't the only man in Thebes trading in stolen goods. Far from it. Greedily, the other man unwrapped the leather cloth and examined the precious objects. This was no stranger. As he turned his face towards Amenpanufer and smiled, a long, snaking scar could be seen across one eye and cheek. This was none other than Bakwerel, the Chief of the Medjay police.

PART TWO

Building a royal tomb

ACROSS THE RIVER NILE, in the Valley of the Kings, work was under way on the tomb of Egypt's ruler, Pharaoh Rameses IX. Here, hidden among the rugged rock faces, was the burial ground of Egypt's greatest warrior-pharaohs, Tuthmosis III and Rameses the Great. And somewhere deep beneath the cliffs lay the two-hundred-year-old tomb of the boy-king, Tutankhamun.

At the entrance to the tomb, a group of workmen were passing the time of day. The great pyramids of Egypt's Old Kingdom rulers had proved too much of a target for tomb robbers. Now only a plain doorway cut into the rock marked the entrance to the Pharaoh's eventual burial place. The tomb was being built in secret and only a carefully chosen band of workmen were allowed into the valley.

A young boy, the painter's son, carrying a goatskin flask of water, walked through the doorway and into a long passage. The tomb stretched for over a hundred metres into the cliff face. A line of workmen stumbled past in the opposite direction, hauling heavy sacks of rubble. In the first two years of building alone, over three thousands tonnes of rock had been hacked

THE VALLEY OF THE KINGS

For centuries the Pharaohs of Egypt were buried in massive, pyramid-shaped tombs. The slanting sides represented the sun's rays, up which the Pharaoh's soul could climb to reach the sun god, Re. But the pyramids were regularly plundered, so the Pharaohs of the New Kingdom chose tombs cut deep into the sides of cliffs. These were in a valley on the West Bank of Thebes, the Valley of the Kings. The tombs had a central corridor or tunnel, leading to the main burial chamber with smaller rooms off it. From outside the entrances were hard to see, but inside they were lavishly decorated with paintings of the Pharaohs' journeys through the afterlife. The Valley was hard to reach but, despite tight security, the tombs were not safe for long.

away. The passage was lit by hundreds of flickering oil lamps. Both sides of the walls were covered in wooden scaffolding, on which the men worked. The heat was stifling and the air was filled with choking plaster and stone dust. But the atmosphere was lively, and the men laughed and chatted as they went about their work. These men were the greatest craftsmen and artists of their day, hand-picked and trained to provide a fitting setting for the Pharaoh's journey through the afterlife. The painter's son handed the flask to a workman, plastering the stone walls. Like all the other men, he was dripping with sweat, and took a long, thirsty swig.

Secrets and suspicions

OVER SIXTY MEN WORKED IN TWO GANGS, each responsible for one side of the tomb. Not surprisingly, in a country dominated by the River Nile, the gangs were organised into 'left' and 'right', like the crew of an Egyptian warship. Each gang answered to a captain who oversaw and checked their work.

Pentaweret, the painter, was busy completing a colourful figure of the Pharaoh. In one hand, he held a small sketch drawn on a fragment of limestone. The sketch was divided up by a grid of squares. Frowning with concentration, Pentaweret consulted the sketch, then copied one square of the grid on to the larger squares already printed in red on the plaster wall. It was painstaking work, and it was vital to get it right. A Pharaoh's tomb could take over fifty years to complete – more than a lifetime for the tomb-builders, who would be lucky to live beyond forty. From an early age, their sons were trained to take over their fathers' jobs. Pentaweret paused to drink from his son's flask. Then he went back to his work. Next to him another workman wiped his eyes, squinting in the smokey gloom. To reduce the smoke from their lamps, the tomb builders added salt to the oil, but this made the lamps less bright. Going blind was every tomb painter's worst fear.

The day drew to a close. As darkness fell, a shout came from the tomb doorway.

"Time to go home," called Harshire, the tombs' chief scribe, consulting his sun clock. "That's all for today."

The goverment had no wish to overwork its valuable

employees. Officially, their working day was limited to eight hours. But Egyptian time-keeping did not always work in the tomb-builders' favour. An Egyptian week was ten days long. Daylight was divided into twelve equal segments, so an hour changed length according to the time of the year. At the height of the summer, an eight-hour day was nine hours and twenty minutes long. Special scribes were on hand to supervise the tomb-builders' daily progress. But Harshire, the chief scribe, also had another function...

Harshire and his team of scribes watched the tomb-builders' every move. As the workmen left the tomb, they handed over their tools to the scribes to be checked. After all, they were entrusted with the greatest secrets in Egypt. Not only did they know where the Pharaoh's bodies were buried, but where their treasure was, too. Every tool was checked in to make sure they were not used in robberies. The authorities did not trust their valued craftsmen. With good reason. Harshire recorded every person who entered the Valley, and ticked them off as they left. Anything unusual or suspicious was immediately reported to the authorities.

After checking in his tools, Pentaweret and the captain of his gang sauntered over to a small hut a short distance from the tomb. Peering up from his writing, Harshire watched them closely. Just then he heard someone call his name. He turned round to see Pawero, accompanied by two Medjay guards.

"So, Harshire," Pawero, said, smiling smugly, "How is it all going?"

Pawero, the Mayor of West Thebes, was Harshire's boss. He had overall authority for the West Bank of Thebes, with responsibility for the security of the royal tombs. In this, he was ably backed up by the Medjay, the Theban police. But before Harshire could answer, Pawero walked over to the hut from which Pentaweret emerged, clutching a bag. To Harshire's surprise, the two men exchanged a few words. He could not hear what was being said but he had his own idea. Despite the tight security, Harshire had begun to have suspicions about what was going on in the Valley of the Kings.

The place of truth

DURING THE WEEK, the tomb-builders lived in temporary lodgings near their work site in the Valley of the Kings. But at the weekend, the men set off home to their wives and families for a two day holiday.

The steep, rocky path leading out of the Valley was closely guarded by the Medjay police. As many as one hundred and twenty Medjay patrolled the royal tombs – twice the number of the tomb-builders. No one was allowed to enter or leave the Valley without their permission. Now, as Pentaweret and the other tomb-builders left their lodgings, they knew they were being watched. The sun was setting as they climbed the path to the top of the hill, and saw below them, in the next steep-sided valley, smoke rising from the houses of their village. All the tomb-builders lived in the same village. It was called Set Ma'at, "The Place of Truth" (now called Deir el-Medina).

Passing the Medjay guards at the gate, Pentaweret and the

TOMB TREASURES

The ancient Egyptians believed that, after death, a person's soul travelled to the next world, called the Kingdom of the West. Wealthy Egyptians were mummified, to preserve their souls for the afterlife, and were placed in magnificent gilded and painted wooden coffins. Within the mummy's wrappings were semi-precious stones. Their tombs were filled with objects to make the afterlife comfortable, such as food, clothes, weapons, jewellery and furniture. Buried with them were hundreds of small figures, called ushabtis, who would travel to the next world with them as servants. Poor Egyptians were usually buried in holes in the desert sand or in small, simple tombs cut into the ground.

captain walked into the village along a narrow, sandy street. The street was lined with neatly painted houses, their doorways edged in red. Thirsty after their journey, the two men stopped to drink from a large water jar in the street. Unseen by them, Harshire was standing some distance away and could hear them whispering. Then they parted, and Pentaweret soon reached his house where his wife and children were waiting to greet him. His son was already at home and was sitting on the stairs, painting with a fine brush on a piece of pottery. He was practising writing hieroglyphs. His father looked over his shoulder and smiled.

Life was comfortable for the tomb-builders. In return for their skills, all their needs were taken care of by the authorities. Their wages were paid in food, fuel and other goods, and the Pharaoh provided slaves to grind the villagers' grain. Most of the villagers were educated, and they were given plenty of free time. But underneath this well-ordered existence, some of the tomb-builders were involved in another line of business.

Royal smugglers

WITHOUT SAYING A WORD, Pentaweret beckoned his wife to follow him into the living room. He pulled something from his work bag which his wife quickly wrapped in the cloth she was carrying. For behind closed doors, Pentaweret and several other families were using their privileged positions to plunder the West Bank tombs. The Place of Truth was stuffed with stolen treasure. After all, they were well placed to rob the tombs. And the poor harvests and rising grain prices affecting Thebes were being felt in Deir el-Medina, too. Over the last three months, their food supplies had failed to arrive several times. And, each time, the whole workforce went on strike until their rations were delivered. But it wasn't really poverty that drove the tomb-builders to crime. It seemed that the temptation of all that sacred treasure buried in the hills where they worked was just too hard to resist.

Suddenly, there was a knock at the door, and Pentaweret and his wife looked up in alarm. But it was only the captain, carrying a basket covered in a cloth. The captain lifted the cloth and pulled out several fabulous, gilded figures and jewels to show to Pentaweret. The painter's eyes lit up. They packed the objects back into the basket, then Pentaweret opened a wooden chest, crammed full with more treasures, which he emptied into another basket.

Later that evening, under cover of darkness, the painter and his son carried the two baskets up the stairs to the roof. Pentaweret passed his basket over the low wall to where a woman was waiting. Then his son climbed over the wall and followed the woman across the rooftops. Making sure there

DEIR EL-MEDINA

The royal tomb-builders lived in the village of Deir el-Medina, built specially for them by the Egyptian government. Its remote desert location meant that the workmen could be watched at all times. The village was abandoned at the end of the New Kingdom. In the twentieth century, excavations showed that the main street was lined with about 68 small, mud-brick houses. The whole village was surrounded by a wall. The only road to the village was closely guarded. There was no real reason for the villagers to leave. The government provided them with all they needed to live quite comfortably.

45

were no guards about, the painter's son gave a low whistle. A little way up the street, a man with a donkey was waiting. Quickly and quietly, the woman and the painter's son hoisted their baskets over the wall. They covered them with dirty washing and loaded them on to the donkey. Then the painter's son jumped on its back, gave the donkey a tap and set off down the street, trotting past the guards at the village gates without even a second glance.

This wasn't just petty pilfering. Several of the families were running an extremely profitable racket. Treasure stolen from the tombs during the week was brought back to the village. From there, it was smuggled to waiting customers in towns up and down the River Nile. But one man had realised what was going on. From a doorway further down the street, Harshire, the chief scribe, watched the painter's son leave the village. He had seen the whole thing. And he decided to do his duty, and put a stop to the scandal.

PART THREE

The plot thickens

A FEW DAYS LATER, HARSHIRE, THE CHIEF SCRIBE, walked nervously up to a grand and imposing house in East Thebes. He had thought long and hard about what to do, and had decided to tell the authorities about his suspicions. He should have reported them to his boss, Pawero, the mayor of West Thebes, but it seemed that he did not trust his master.

Instead he had come to the house of Paser, the mayor of East Thebes, Pawero's arch rival. And, without realising it, he had set in motion a sequence of events that would seal the fate of the quarryman, Amenpanufer.

In the sumptuous sitting room of his luxurious home, Paser was playing a game of Senet with his ten-year-old son. Father and son were sitting on either side of a small table and were laughing as they moved their counters.

Paser's wife relaxed in a chair while a servant manicured her nails. Paser was a wealthy man, and liked to be surrounded by the fine things in life. But he was also extremely pious, and the journey to the afterlife affected every aspect of his life. Even the board game Senet was based on the journey to the next world. Just then a servant came in.

"Master, someone is at the door," he told Paser. "And he is asking to see you."

It was late in the evening and Paser was not expecting visitors. But he told the servant to send the man in. Looking flustered, Harshire was ushered into the room, bowing and apologising for disturbing the mayor's evening.

"Never mind all that," said Paser, impatiently. "Sit down and tell me what you want."

So Harshire began to tell his story...

As the treacherous tale unfolded, Paser looked more and more horrified. Strictly speaking, as mayor of East Thebes, Paser had no authority over the West Bank tombs, but these were serious charges which he could not ignore. Before taking the matter to the Vizier, Paser decided to take matters into his own hands and conduct his own undercover investigation. He could hardly have forseen the extent of the plundering.

A scapegoat

BUT PASER'S INVESTIGATION did not stay secret for long. When he heard what his rival was planning to do, Pawero was furious. After all, it would not look good for the mayor of West Thebes if news of the scandal was to get out and reach the Vizier's ears. But how much did Pawero already know about the tomb-robbing racket in the village? Was he himself involved? The evidence suggests that he was. To protect his own back, he decided that the only course of action was to divert attention away from the village... and his own part in the dreadful crime. And he knew just the person to help him – Bakwerel, the chief of the Medjay police. But for his plan to work, he needed to frame someone else for the crime...

Amenpanufer was at home, sitting with his wife and their tiny baby. Suddenly, their peace was shattered. Without warning, the door was flung open and Bakwerel burst in, followed by several Medjay. Despite his wife's pleading and his children's terrified screams, Amenpanufer was arrested and dragged roughly out of the house. Bakwerel ordered him to be taken away and thrown into a prison cell in the Temple of Karnak. It seemed to the quarryman that his four-year old crime had come back to haunt him. Pawero had found his scapegoat. The trial of Amenpanufer would distract everyone's attention from Paser's investigation.

A full confession

THE MAGNIFICENT TEMPLE OF KARNAK, dedicated to the god Amun-Re, was not only the most sacred site in Egypt, it was also a courtroom. But this was no ordinary case. Amenpanufer was accused of a crime so serious that the Vizier himself, the Pharaoh's Prime Minister, had been called in to interrogate him. Outside the royal family, the Vizier was the most important man in Egypt. He was the Pharaoh's second-in-command, responsible for collecting taxes, managing the royal coffers and organising the lives of thousands of ordinary Egyptians. Now he was being called upon in his most important role – as the highest judge in the land. In the Great Hypostyle Hall at Karnak, Pawero greeted the Vizier and explained what had happened. Things looked bleak for Amenpanufer. The humble quarryman was about to come face to face with the full force of Egyptian law.

In his dingy prison cell, Amenpanufer was dragged to his feet by a Medjay guard. For a split second, he caught Bakwerel's gaze and the two men glared at each other. Then the door burst open and the Vizier marched in. As the guard forced Amenpanufer to kneel, the Vizier looked in disgust at the broken man at his feet. Amenpanufer had been accused of the worst crime imaginable. When the Pharaohs died, they were honoured as gods. To rob and disturb their tombs was to upset the natural order of things, and bring chaos and destruction to the land. This wasn't just robbery, this was a crime against the gods. The task now facing the Vizier was to establish

THE TEMPLE OF KARNAK

The magnificent Temple of Karnak in East Thebes is the largest religious building ever constructed. The sacred precinct of Amun-Re alone would have held ten cathedrals. The temple was dedicated to Amun-Re, the most powerful Theban god. It was built by successive Pharaohs, each eager to make his mark. The Great Hypostyle Hall, with its 134 painted columns, was added by Pharaoh Rameses II. To the north of the precinct of Amun-Re lay the precinct of Montu. It was here that Amenpanufer was tortured. His trial was also held in the Temple, probably in the First Court.

Amenpanufer's innocence or guilt. And ancient Egyptian justice had its own painful way of extracting information from suspects. The Vizier began his interrogation by barking an order:

"Let the torture begin," he hissed.

Amenpanufer was beaten, then his hands were tied behind his back and bound to a plank of wood. As the two Medjay turned the plank round, Amenpanufer's face twisted in agony. Torture was an accepted part of interrogation, and it rarely took long to extract a confession. As usual, a scribe was on hand to record Amenpanufer's words. These have survived to this day, along with records of his trial.

His body wracked with terrible pain, Amenpanufer began:
"I went beyond the Fortress to the West of Thebes as I
usually did. I was with seven other men..."

Tour of the tombs

ON A RUGGED HILLSIDE IN WEST THEBES, a badly
beaten Amenpanufer, flanked by Pawero and Bakwerel, was
dragged along behind the Vizier by two Medjay guards. By the
fourth day of his interrogation, an exhausted Amenpanufer had
made a full confession to the robbery of the tomb of Pharaoh
Sobekemsaf II, who had been buried over three hundred years
earlier on the West Bank of the Nile. The group stopped by an
opening roughly cut into the rock, and the Medjay, led by
Bakwerel, squeezed inside. As part of his trial, Amenpanufer
was led to the scene of his crime. Conveniently, it lay outside
the Valley of the Kings, well away from the tomb-builders'
village. Bakwerel and the Medjay emerged from the hole and
reported back to the Vizier. There seemed to be no doubt about
it – Amenpanufer was guilty as charged.

While Amenpanufer was led away, Pawero took the Vizier
and Bakwerel in the opposite direction, along a high path. To
reassure the Vizier that none of the other tombs had been
tampered with, Pawero took him on a tour of inspection. No
wonder the Vizier was satisfied. For Pawero had made doubly
sure that anything suspicious had been covered up. He and
Bakwerel exchanged a look of triumph. Their plan was working

brilliantly. The Vizier did not suspect a thing. Now all that remained was for Amenpanufer to be sentenced and their secret would be safe.

A dangerous celebration

NEXT EVENING, IN PENTAWERET'S HOUSE, the painter, his son and the captain celebrated: Amenpanufer was to be punished for his earlier crime, and no one had realised they themselves were robbing tombs. Knowing that an investigation was going on, the tomb robbers had kept a close eye on events. The day after Pawero's tour of the tombs, word reached them that the quarryman was to be sentenced in front of the Great Court. Better still, the Vizier had found no evidence of any other robberies. Now the real tomb robbers were celebrating – they were off the hook. The beer flowed freely and soon they were all very drunk. So drunk they thought it would be a fine idea to cross the river to East Thebes and carry on the rejoicing there. Clinging on to each other for support, the rowdy group set off out of the village.

Hearing the sounds of drunken jeers and catcalls outside his house, Paser woke up with a start. He frowned, and climbed up to the roof to see what all the noise was about. Beneath him, Pentaweret and his friends stood unsteadily on the street corner, shouting insults. We do not know exactly why they ended up outside Paser's house. Perhaps they felt untouchable now that the Vizier had wrapped up the case, or perhaps they were simply drunk. Whatever the reason, it was not a wise move to mock the very man who had been investigating them. Paser was in no mood for insults. He looked down from his roof terrace and shouted back at them.

"What are you doing here?" he called. "Come on, explain yourselves."

"Don't you know?" sneered the captain, to loud cheers. "No one can touch the kings who lie in the Valley. They are safe in their tombs for ever. At least, that's what the Vizier says."

At that moment, Paser realised the tomb-builders thought they had got away with their crimes. Spurred on by their taunting, he decided to let them into a secret.

"I wouldn't be so sure," he said, menacingly. "Your own scribe, Harshire, has been to see me with five serious charges against you. I will be taking the matter to the Pharaoh and asking him to send his own people to deal with you."

The foolish tomb-builders should have stayed at home and kept their mouths firmly shut. Now they had spurred the mayor of East Thebes into action. But, unusually, Paser had decided not to take his case to the Vizier, his superior in Thebes. Instead, he went above the Vizier's head, straight to the Pharaoh. It was a mistake he would bitterly regret.

Unseen by Paser and the tomb robbers, Pawero and Bakwerel had been hiding in the shadows, listening to every word. A delighted Pawero could not believe his luck. Here was a chance to get back at his rival, *and* to protect his own neck. Threatening to go straight to the Pharaoh went against all the rules. The Vizier would not take kindly to this insult to his authority. So, when he got home, scheming Pawero decided to write a letter to the Vizier, telling him exactly what he had heard.

Betrayed by a letter

THE FOLLOWING DAY, the letter reached the Vizier. Sure enough, it had exactly the effect Pawero had hoped it would. It was a baking hot day in Thebes. The Vizier sat on a stool in the shade while his barber shaved him and rubbed oil into his head, ready for his elaborate wig. By his side stood his scribe, Nesamun, reading Pawero's letter aloud:

"I heard him talking to the men of West Thebes... I could not make sense of the grave accusations but I cannot keep silent about them. I am therefore reporting these charges to you which Mayor Paser said he would report directly to the Pharaoh. I place them before my lord to be investigated immediately."

As the scribe reached the end of the letter, the astonished Vizier got up from his stool, calling for his wig, and rushed off in a fury. He was much more concerned about the insult to his authority than Paser's charges against the tomb-builders. After all, the last thing he wanted was for the Pharaoh to be brought in over his head. That would make him look weak and stupid. And so the plot thickened. A case of tomb-robbing had become a political time-bomb. And the show trial of Amenpanufer now took on a new political meaning.

Amenpanufer cowered in a corner of his cell. He'd been

badly beaten and was covered in bruises. He barely had the strength to look up when the door crashed open and he was ordered to stand.

PART FOUR

The trial begins

ON THE SIXTH DAY OF THE INVESTIGATION, the Great Court met in the Temple of Karnak. In the early morning, the officials gathered. They included the High Priest, wearing a leopard skin over his tunic, and the mayors of West and East Thebes – Pawero smug and pleased with himself; Paser pale and anxious, whispering nervously to Harshire. When the officials were seated, two guards dragged a bruised and battered man through the doorway and made him stand before the Vizier. In the Great Court, the Vizier was the prosecutor, judge and jury. As he took his seat, he gave Paser a cold look.

Amenpanufer glanced around the temple courtyard. This would be the first and only time a man like Amenpanufer would have walked through the halls of Karnak. Ordinary people were not allowed to enter the sacred home of Amun-Re. As the quarryman stepped before the court, the scribe read out the list of accusations against him. Then it was Amenpanufer's turn. Every trial began with an oath:

"If I tell lies, may I be mutilated and sent into exile," he recited.

But this was not a cross-examination. As far as the court

was concerned, Amenpanufer's confession had already established his guilt. All the court needed now was a public confession before they passed sentence. The Vizier addressed Amenpanufer:

"Name the thieves who were with you."

There was silence. Then, slowly and haltingly, Amenpanufer began his confession...

"I was employed with other stonemasons, and I fell into the habit of robbing the tombs..."

King Sobekemsaf's tomb

AMENPANUFER'S CONFESSION WENT ON... One night, he and his gang climbed the hill to the royal tombs. Finding the tomb of King Sobekemsaf, they began to chisel their way through the rock face with their copper tools. They broke into the back of the tomb, partly to avoid detection and partly to avoid the curses carved on the tomb door. Once inside, they hacked a hole through a wall, into the king's burial chamber, the innermost part of the tomb.

By the light of their flickering candles, the men looked around in awe. Scenes of the Pharaoh in the afterlife were painted on the walls. The tomb was full of fabulous furniture, chariots, chests, gilded shrines and statues of the gods. Treasure beyond their wildest dreams. But the greatest treasure of all was the golden coffin of King Sobekemsaf, buried around four hundred and fifty years before. Like all Egyptians, the men recognised the dead king as a god. But that didn't stop them breaking into his coffin and trashing his tomb. Inside they found the king's mummy, decorated with glittering jewels and golden amulets, his face covered with a golden death mask.

In a frenzy, the men began stuffing treasures into sacks. They would share the loot out later. Some dragged the king's mummy out of its coffin and set the coffin on fire. As the fire took hold, the gold covering the coffin melted and formed pools on the floor. When this cooled and hardened, the men collected it up. It would fetch a high price on the Theban black market. Then, with a backward glance at the devastated tomb, Amenpanufer followed his companions out through the hole in the wall.

Passing sentence

A HUSH FELL ON THE COURTROOM. As Amenpanufer finished his confession, Pawero glanced at Bakwerel and raised his eyebrows.

"Well, there we are," he whispered. "All sorted."

The Vizier rose to his feet. All that remained was for him to pass sentence on Amenpanufer. But that was not the first thing on the Vizier's mind. First, he had to deal with Paser. With a look of triumph on his face, he pointed at the unfortunate mayor.

"This man made certain accusations against the tomb-builders," he bellowed. "Yet when I inspected the tombs, I did

LAW AND ORDER

Each Egyptian town had its own local court but cases of national importance were heard by the Great Court, presided over by the Vizier, who acted as jury and lawyer. Amenpanufer was not cross-examined because the court had already decided he was guilty. Trials were carried out in the name of Ma'at, goddess of truth and justice, who upheld order and harmony. The Vizier and other officials probably wore a gold pendant of Ma'at around their necks as a badge of office. For Egyptians a serious crime like tomb-robbing caused a breakdown in ma'at. To restore order and avoid chaos, it was essential for justice to be done.

not find anything untoward. Everything he said has turned out to be false."

For the Vizier had decided to turn Amenpanufer's trial into an opportunity to humiliate the Mayor of East Thebes. Looking smug, the Vizier sat down. Paser shook his head in frustration, then stood up and opened his mouth to speak. But before he could utter a word, another voice rang out loudly in the courtroom. Angrily, the Vizier turned to stare at Amenpanufer, for the voice belonged to the quarryman. Despite the guards' efforts to silence him, Amenpanufer carried on speaking. His confession was not quite over. Certain now of his fate, he decided that he had more to say. After all, he had nothing to lose. He began to list the officials he had bribed to keep quiet.

"I took my share of twenty gold coins, and gave them to the scribe. He released me without question," he shouted, as the guards tried to gag him. "That's how we were able to carry on robbing the tombs. And it wasn't just us. There are people among you who are as guilty as we are. They know who they are."

Amenpanufer's words caused uproar. Nervously, the Vizier fiddled with the pendant of Ma'at around his neck, while Pawero and Bakwerel exchanged guilty glances. As many in the courtroom knew, the truth was uncomfortable to hear. Unfortunately for Amenpanufer, it would do nothing to save his skin.

A scandal uncovered

HIS HANDS TIED BEHIND HIS BACK, Amenpanufer was led through the marketplace in Thebes, followed by his fellow tomb robbers. Jeering crowds lined the streets to watch them pass. Among them was Amenpanufer's wife. In despair, she rushed forward to plead for her husband's life, but the guards pushed her back. For Amenpanufer, the cruellest punishment in Egyptian law lay in store. He could expect to have no tomb as a resting place and no grave goods to help him on his journey through the afterlife.

Leaving the marketplace, the terrified tomb robbers were

dragged up a barren, rocky path to a desert hillside. Ahead, they could see a row of dark shapes silhouetted in the harsh midday sun. As they got closer, a gruesome scene emerged. The shapes were half-rotten bodies impaled on tall, wooden spikes. This was the place of execution. As a lesson to all those tempted to disturb the Pharaohs' peace, Amenpanufer had been sentenced to a slow, agonising death. Worse still, their mutilated bodies would not be buried and so would not reach the afterlife. For an ancient Egyptian, this was a fate worse than death.

But that was not the end of the story. A year later, the Vizier finally launched a full-scale investigation to clear up the tomb-robbing scandal. In Deir el-Medina, eight of the tomb robbers, including Pentaweret, were arrested and interrogated. Their houses were raided by the Medjay, and their families brutally tortured. Their confessions uncovered the true extent of the scandal, and each of the accused shared the same grisly fate as the quarryman. Stolen goods from the royal tombs were found in houses all over Thebes, even in the homes of the wealthy and powerful, and gold, silver and bronze, precious oils and sacred cloth were recovered from towns miles away. The black market had spread far and wide, all along the River Nile.

Even so, Paser, the man who had uncovered the scandal, got no thanks for his role. He disappeared from the records and probably lost his job. And who did the Vizier appoint to clean up the sacred city? None other than Pawero. But tomb-robbing continued to be a thorn in the side of the Theban authorities, and some years later the mummies of the New Kingdom pharaohs were taken from the Valley of the Kings and secretly buried, without any treasure, in a cave hidden high in the Theban hills. Modern tomb robbers rediscovered them in the nineteenth century, and today they can be seen in the Egyptian Museum in Cairo .

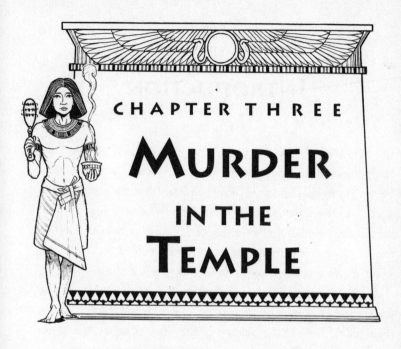

CHAPTER THREE

MURDER IN THE TEMPLE

Main characters in the story:

Psamtek I (*Sam-Teck*) – *Pharaoh of Egypt*

Petiese (*Pet-ee-essay*) – *a close relative of Psamtek*

Nitemhe (*Nitt-em-hay*) – *daughter of Petiese; Horudj's wife*

Horudj (*Ho [hot]-roodge*) – *priest of Amun; Nitemhe's husband*

Ibi (*Ib-ee*) – *son of Nitemhe and Horudj*

Karem (*Car-em*) – *son of Nitemhe and Horudj*

Samut (*Sam-mut*) – *priest of Amun*

INTRODUCTION

IN 1069BC, RAMESSES XI, the last Pharaoh of the New Kingdom, died. His death marked the beginning of centuries of turmoil in Egypt, and civil unrest spread from the south to the north. Invaders from Libya swept into the delta. Temples and tombs were looted of their treasures. Nubian princes conquered the south and founded their own kingdom. For four hundred years, Egypt was torn apart into warring provinces.

During this time, with no central authority to answer to, the priesthood of Amun-Re went from strength to strength. From their power base in the Temple of Karnak in Thebes, they held on to their wealth, and kept control of the vast estates they had once administered for the Pharaoh. Then, in the seventh century BC, Psamtek, a warlord from Sais in the north, seized the vacant throne of Egypt. Years of invasion and foreign rule had left Egypt weak, poor and divided. Without delay, Pharaoh Psamtek I pushed the Nubians out of Egypt and set about reuniting the country and restoring peace and prosperity. But trouble was brewing. Psamtek's efforts to establish himself as a strong ruler were to bring him head to head with the priests of Amun.

It was perhaps as well for an Egyptian woman named Nitemhe that she could not forsee how this conflict would affect her and her family: that she would find herself weeping in the courtyard of her home, the bodies of her two young sons before her. For Nitemhe and her family, the struggle for control of Egypt would end in terrible tragedy – the death of her two young sons. It would lead to a bitter and bloody feud which would destroy one of Egypt's most powerful families.

PART ONE

Power struggle

IN THE TOWN OF TEUDJOI, on the east bank of the River Nile in Middle Egypt, the day began like any other. The town was built on a limestone hill above the fertile river plain. Here farmers were hard at work in the fields, as they had done for centuries. Ancient Egypt's civilisation and wealth was based on the crops that grew in these fields, watered by the mighty river. It was the income from these crops that paid for Egypt's magnificent pyramids, temples and tombs. Whoever controlled the land controlled Egypt.

But the day was about to take an alarming turn. In the distance, through the heat haze, a group of men marched into the town. In the centre was a stern-looking man, surrounded by armed soldiers and scribes. Alarmed, the townspeople scattered in panic and let the strangers pass. They did not want any trouble. The man in the middle of the group was called Petiese, a close relative of the new Pharaoh. It was four years since

Psamtek had seized power, and he had given Petiese a key post in his new government. His job was to put the priests of Amun firmly back in their place. In 660BC, Petiese arrived in Teudjoi to do the Pharaoh's bidding.

Trouble in the temple

WITH NO ONE STANDING IN THEIR WAY, the men marched straight into the courtyard of the Great Temple of Amun. The town was a stronghold of the priests of Amun, and its temple owned vast areas of Egypt's precious farmland.

"Search the temple," Petiese barked at the soldiers. "And make sure you're thorough about it. I want to know exactly what's been going on here."

For years, the temples of Egypt had looked after the Pharaoh's lands. But over the last few centuries, with no one to question them, the priests of Amun had taken control of the land for themselves and grown rich on the profits. Now, the new Pharaoh was ready to stamp his authority. He wanted the lands, and their profits, back, and he sent Petiese to get them for him.

In the temple, Petiese and the soldiers searched every storeroom and counted every sack of grain. Then they entered the great hall. The doors to the sanctuary were firmly closed, but hearing the commotion, two priests had hidden behind the pillars. Great temples usually had dozens of priests to serve their gods, but not in Teudjoi. Here Petiese only found these two priests – an old man, and a teenager called Samut. There

66

KING OF THE GODS

The ancient Egyptians worshipped hundreds of gods and goddesses. One of the most important gods was Amun. In the New Kingdom, Amun was the king of the gods. He was linked with Re, the sun god, or creator, and became known as Amun-Re. Each Pharaoh was believed to be Amun-Re's son. Amun-Re's main temple was at Karnak in Thebes, but he was worshipped throughout Egypt in smaller temples and shrines. The priests who served in his temples grew very powerful indeed. Many Egyptian deities were identified with particular animals. Amun-Re was sometimes shown in statues and carvings with a ram's head.

was no escape for them. Stony-faced, Petiese ordered the soldiers to seize them, then they were dragged away and badly beaten. As Samut cowered in a corner in agony, a deep, red gash across his forehead, Petiese interrogated the old priest about what payments were due to the Pharaoh.

With this brutal show of strength, Petiese succeeded in bringing the Temple of Amun once more under the Pharaoh's control. From here, the message that the Pharaoh was back in charge would soon spread to the priests at Thebes. But in doing the Pharaoh's dirty work, Petiese also sowed the seeds of his own family's downfall.

Family affairs

ELEVEN YEARS HAD PASSED since Petiese first arrived in Teudjoi, and he was now one of the richest and most powerful men in Egypt. In the past few years, he had travelled up and down the Nile, bringing temple after temple back under the Pharaoh's control. In doing so, he had doubled the income flowing from the temples into the royal coffers. Petiese himself had grown rich on his share of the profits from the Temple of Amun in Teudjoi, where he lived in a grand and beautiful house with his wife and four children. His three sons were his pride and joy. For in Egypt, sons were valuable. After all, they would be responsible for providing their father with a lavish burial to ensure that he enjoyed a comfortable afterlife in the next world.

But Petiese also had a daughter, called Nitemhe, who was fifteen years old – old enough to get married. For a man with Petiese's wealth and position, his daughter's marriage could be a very useful way of furthering his own career.

Temple rituals

DAY WAS JUST BEGINNING IN THE TEMPLE OF AMUN. In the darkened sanctuary, two priests stepped solemnly forward and opened the door of the shrine. The temple was now firmly under Petiese's control. But one of the shrine openers had not forgotten Petiese's past. Samut's forehead was marked by a jagged white scar – a reminder of a savage beating.

For now, though, Samut concentrated on his priestly duties. Every morning the god Amun was woken by his priests. Samut began to chant the morning prayer:

"Praise to Amun-Re, Lord of Thrones-of-the-two-lands, the great god. Kissing the ground to Amun of Thebes, the great god, the Lord of this Sanctuary, great and fair, that he may let my eyes see his beauty."

Then Petiese himself stepped into the sanctuary, dressed in his priestly finery. He sprinkled water on the statue of Amun, while other priests brought offerings of oil, beer, incense, herbs and honey and presented them to the god. Daily offerings guaranteed the god's goodwill and help in times of trouble. Another priest dressed the statue in a crisp white linen cloak. Petiese was now the Prophet of Amun, a title of great honour bestowed on him by the Pharaoh. In addition, Psamtek rewarded his faithful servant with a fifth of the income from the temple lands. This was twenty times more than any other priest in Teudjoi. Petiese was a very rich man indeed.

Arranging a wedding

LATER THAT DAY, BACK AT HIS HOME, Petiese had a visitor. It was a young priest called Horudj, whom Petiese had summoned from Thebes. Generations before, Horudj's ancestors had been priests in Teudjoi, and now he wanted to claim his rightful place in the Temple of Amun. The two men seemed to get on like a house on fire.

"As we agreed, I will pay off your debts and find you a post in the Temple of Amun," said Petiese. "And in return, you will be my eyes and ears. Do you understand?"

"Perfectly," replied Horudj, with a smile.

Just at that moment, Nitemhe came into the room with a jug of wine. She greeted Horudj politely as she poured the wine out. For his part, Horudj could not take his eyes off her, but it wasn't a matter of love at first sight. Here he saw the perfect opportunity to tie his own fortunes in with those of one of Egypt's most prestigious families.

"Would you do me the honour of letting me marry your

GETTING MARRIED

In ancient Egypt girls from poor families got married when they were as young as 12 years old. Girls from richer families were often a few years older. The marriage was usually arranged by the couple's families. There was no wedding ceremony as far as we know but wealthy couples signed a marriage contract stating their goods and property, and what would happen to these if the couple divorced or one of them died. Women in Egypt were much better off than elsewhere in the ancient world. They could own property, had many of the same rights as men, and, like Nitemhe, ran their farms and businesses when their husbands were away.

daughter?" he asked Petiese, when Nitemhe had left the room.

"If you become my representative in the Temple, you can marry her with my blessing," replied Petiese.

And so the deal was done. Shortly afterwards, Horudj married Nitemhe. For Petiese, this marriage was also a blessing, a way of keeping his affairs in the family and of making plans for his retirement. For Horudj, it was a step up in the world, just as he had hoped. Through his marriage to Nitemhe, he was now Petiese's right-hand man in the temple. But there were troubled times ahead. His new position soon brought him into conflict with the other priests, including Samut, who resented his high-handed ways. In return, Horudj didn't trust the priests an inch. But, when he tried to complain to his father-in-law, Petiese dropped a bombshell.

"I am an old man," Petiese told him. "And I want to retire. So I have asked the Pharaoh to allow me to leave his service. I shall go to live in Thebes with my wife and sons. But I want you to stay here in Teudjoi and collect my taxes for me."

Horudj was horrified at what he heard. Without Petiese's influence, he was afraid that he would not have the authority to control the other priests. But Petiese would hear none of it and assured him that he had nothing to fear.

"The Pharaoh will protect you," he told his son-in-law.

Some time later, Nitemhe watched sadly as her father, mother, brothers and their servants got ready to leave. Without her family for company, and married to a husband she had not chosen for herself, she suddenly felt very lonely. As her family set off, Nitemhe rushed forward and grabbed her father's hand.

"Take me to Thebes with you," she pleaded. "I beg you, please don't leave me."

"No, daughter," said Petiese, firmly. "You will have a much better life here."

And leaving Nitemhe sobbing, they set off for their new home.

PART TWO

Rich and poor

SEVENTEEN YEARS HAD PASSED since Petiese left Teudjoi to begin his new life in Thebes. In the Temple of Teudjoi, Horudj had taken over his father-in-law's role as the Pharaoh's representative. Across the whole of Upper Egypt, an understanding between the Pharaoh and the priests of Amun had gradually been reached. But some old scores had still not been settled...

When they weren't carrying out their duties in the temple, the priests of Amun managed the temple lands and the royal estates. The temple collected most of the harvest from the lands, then shared it out – part to the Pharaoh and part to the temple for its own upkeep and to pay the priests' salaries. Some land was rented to farmers who had to pay a third of their harvest in taxes. Priests also had their own plots of land which helped to boost their income. Away from the temple, in

TEMPLE RITUALS

For ancient Egyptians, the temple was the deity's home on Earth. Each temple was dedicated to a particular god or goddess. Their statue was kept in a shrine in the sanctuary, and was 'woken up', dressed and given food each day like a living person. It also recieved offerings at midday and sunset. The Egyptians believed that these rituals were essential to preserve the harmony of the world. Beyond the sanctuary was the hypostyle hall, where processions took place, and one or more courtyards. The temple was entered through a gateway, called a pylon. Only the priests and priestesses were allowed inside. Ordinary people prayed at the temple entrance.

the fields, Samut was busy supervising his family as they harvested the wheat. Samut bent down next to his young son, who was tying the stalks of straw into bundles. The day was hot and it was thirsty work. But not every priestly family had to farm its own fields. In the distance, Samut noticed Nitemhe and her two sons walking past. As he wiped the sweat from his brow, he noticed their fine clothes, their jewellery and their servants. For years the priests of Amun had accepted the authority of Petiese and his family. But the priests were beginning to think that it was time for a change.

Shifting power

THE BALANCE OF POWER IN THEBES had shifted in the years since Petiese left Teudjoi. From his headquarters in Sais in the north, Pharaoh Psamtek realised that the priests of Amun were a force to be reckoned with. To control the south and strengthen his rule, he needed their help and cooperation. So he reached an agreement with the priests, and installed his daughter, Nitocris, in the Temple of Karnak as the Wife of the God Amun. This was a way for him to seal his alliance with the priests and keep a firm foothold in Thebes. In the great temple,

RICH AND POOR

In Ancient Egypt, the lives of rich and poor people were very different. A wealthy man, like Horudj, lived in a large and luxurious house. At night, he and his family sat down to a delicious dinner which may have included delicacies such as Nile turtle and hyena meat. Servants waited on them hand and foot. By contrast, ordinary Egyptians lived in small, simple houses. They lived mainly on a diet of bread and beer, with some fish or poultry.

Petiese knelt down before Nitocris. Behind him stood a line of priests, ready to pay their respects to her. Petiese had watched the tide turn. But the new understanding between Sais and Thebes undermined the position and privileges of his family in Teudjoi.

Growing up

PETIESE'S DAUGHTER, NITEMHE, now had two sons, Ibi, aged twelve, and Karem, aged fourteen. Since her father's departure, Nitemhe had grown used to her life in Teudjoi. She and her family were wealthy. She lived in a grand and beautiful house, with servants at her every beck and call. Like most aristocratic Egyptian women, Nitemhe ran a large household. But her house was more than just a home. The extra food and linen cloth which the household produced was traded up and down the Nile. While her husband worked for the Pharaoh and the temple, Nitemhe ran the family business.

But for now, Nitehme had other matters on her mind. Her sons were sitting in the living room with their nursemaid. Nitehme smiled when she saw them. She loved them more that anything but they were growing up fast. According to Egyptian custom, both boys had their heads shaved, except for one plait of hair worn to the side. But Karem had now reached the age of adulthood. With a few gentle words to reassure him, Nitemhe took a knife and cut off his sidelock. His childhood was over and from now on, he was expected to behave like a man. In time, he would inherit his father and grandfather's status and wealth, and all the privileges that went with them.

Priests and plotting

BACK IN TEUDJOI, the grain harvest was being unloaded in the temple courtyard. As Samut stacked up the sacks of wheat, a scribe counted them carefully. Every year, at harvest time, the temple collected up the grain and other produce from the lands around Teudjoi. The temple stores were the treasuries of Egypt. The produce from the Pharaoh's estates was sent by ship to Memphis. Part of the produce from the temple lands was divided out among the priests as their salaries. A scribe counted out the amount owing to each man, then a temple servant helped him to carry it away.

As the son-in-law of Petiese, Horudj was entitled to a fifth of all the temple's share, awarded to his family by the Pharaoh some twenty years before. He swaggered into the temple now to collect his share, accompanied by his son, Karem, several servants and a line of donkeys. In Egypt grain was more valuable than money, and could be traded or bartered for other goods. Horudj's yearly income made him the richest man in Teudjoi, by a very long way. It meant that he could afford a life of luxury for himself and his family. He did not notice that the other priests looked at him with a mixture of resentment and envy. Being a priest brought many benefits – an income, land

and an education. But no other priest in Teudjoi was as wealthy as Horudj. Each year, they saw the crops they had worked hard to grow slipping through their fingers into Horudj's hands. But for now, the priests said and did nothing. Horudj's time would come.

Harvest festival

IN HORUDJ'S HOUSE, the grain was unloaded and poured into grain silos, and the sacks of other produce were stored in the barn. That evening, the family sat down to a sumptuous feast to celebrate the harvest. Afterwards, they gathered around a fire in the courtyard to praise the goddess Renenutet. She was the goddess of plenty, the Lady of the Fertile Fields, who made sure that there was a good harvest and food and wealth for the coming year. It was a happy time for everyone. As Nitemhe chanted Renenutet's praises, she held an ivory wand with the head of a snake in her hand. For Renenutet was also the snake goddess who killed pests that attacked the crops.

Nitehmhe pushed Ibi forward.

"Take down the corn mummy," she whispered.

Ibi climbed up on one of the sacks and took down a small, dusty figure made from woven straw which hung above the silos. Nitemhe handed him a new figure to hang in its place, and the ivory wand to touch it with magic. This new corn mummy would protect the stores and bring good luck in the future. Proudly, Ibi gave the old straw figure to Karem who threw it into the fire. The old corn mummy was burnt and destroyed, along with all the evil and bad luck it had collected over the past year. But the Egyptians had another sacred snake, called Apep. And Apep was a troublemaker...

As Horudj and his family celebrated, Samut and the other priests of Amun were plotting against him. With the new alliance between the Pharaoh and the priests, the Pharaoh's representative no longer had as much power over them as before. They no longer had to do his bidding, or be afraid to cross his path. That night, they met in secret in a storeroom in the temple. The High Priest was the first to speak.

DUTIES OF A PRIEST

In ancient Egypt, priesthood held power and prestige. Each temple had several priests. Top priests had a job for life, living in or near the temple. Large temples also had part-time priests living at home. Duties included tending the statues of the gods, making offerings and saying prayers. Priests also worked in the temple industries, such as brewing, baking and sandal-making. Before starting work, a priest had to wash, shave, cut his nails and put on clean clothes. He also inhaled incense and chewed natron (a type of salt) to cleanse his mind and mouth, to ensure purity before the gods. Priests recieved some of the food and drink offered to the temple, and land to farm.

"We have had enough of this upstart, Horudj, snatching all our hard-earned grain," he said. "It's time to put an end to his privileges. Let's teach him a lesson. One he won't ever forget."

Then it was Samut's turn to speak. He had more cause than most to bear a grudge against Horudj's family, and had never forgotten the beating he had suffered at Petiese's hands. Now it was time to take his revenge. Slowly, he began to outline his plan.

When he had finished, he asked each of the priests a question in turn:

"Will you go along with this? Will you help bring Horudj down?"

"Yes," each of them replied.

PART THREE

The calm before the storm

IN THE BREWERY OF THE TEMPLE OF AMUN, two of the young priests were busy making beer. One ground barley while the other ground wheat. They added cold water to the barley and warm water to the wheat. They heated up the wheat, and stirred both mixtures together. Then they sieved the mixture and left the liquid to ferment. Beer was the most popular drink in Ancient Egypt and it helped to make the temple, and Horudj, very rich indeed. But how long would his good fortune last?

For a long time, the conspiracy against Horudj had been growing and festering. Riches brought power, and Horudj had made many enemies as he enforced the Pharaoh's authority. Now the priests were finally ready to put their plan into action. Samut entered the brewery and called the two young priests aside.

"Everything is ready," he whispered. "Tonight, bring your knives to the courtyard and hide them among the sacks of grain. Then hide yourselves until the morning. Do you understand?"

The two priests nodded. They knew what they had to do.

Meanwhile, in Horudj's fine house, Nitemhe was putting Karem and Ibi to bed. According to Egyptian custom, she drew a circle around their beds to ward off evil spirits. Otherwise, the Egyptians believed that the spirits would steal or kill them in the night, or pour poison into their ears. She looked tenderly at her sleeping children. Her sons were her pride and joy. Little did she know what lay in store.

Duty and death

NEXT DAY, WITH HORUDJ AWAY ON BUSINESS, it fell to Karem, his eldest son, to take on some of his father's responsibilities. This was his chance to prove himself as a grown-up. Karem's first task was to collect the rest of his family's share of the harvest from the temple, and he was determined to do his father proud.

Just after dawn, he set off for the temple, followed by his

younger brother, a servant and five donkeys. At the temple gates, the two boys walked inside while the servant waited outside.

In the courtyard, the boys looked around. It was quieter than usual but everything seemed to be normal. In one corner stood a large pile of sacks of grain. The boys walked over to the High Priest and Samut, who was in charge of sharing out the grain.

"We have come to collect the rest of our share," said Karem, proudly, trying to make his voice sound deep and grown-up.

"We have come to collect our share," repeated Ibi, in a squeak.

The High Priest looked at them long and hard, then shook his head slowly.

"No, little men," he said, threateningly, "I don't think so. Look behind you. We have something else planned for you."

Scared now, Karem and Ibi turned around. Behind them stood three men, brandishing wooden clubs. Then the young priests pulled their knives from the grain and pointed the gleaming tips at the boys.

"Quick," gasped Karem, grabbing his brother's hand. "Run for it!"

Terrified, the two boys fled for their lives. They ran out of the courtyard and through the temple corridors, followed by their would-be attackers. Dodging their way past the young priests, they made a dash for the shrine of Amun, the temple's innermost sanctuary. Surely, there they would be safe... But just as they reached the Sanctuary, the doors were slammed shut. From behind the columns, more priests appeared and surrounded the boys. There was to be no escape for them. Slowly, the three men raised their clubs and began to beat the sons of Horudj to death.

Danger everywhere

IN THE DISTANCE, through the columns, a figure lurked in the shadows, unseen by the priests. It was Horudj's servant, who had grown tired of waiting and come to see what was keeping the boys. Now, his eyes wide with terror, the servant turned and ran. Gasping for breath, he raced through the streets without stopping and burst through the gates of Horudj's house. Nitemhe tried to calm him down.

"Come on," she said, kindly. "Sit down here and catch your breath. Then you can tell me all about it. It can't be as urgent as all that!"

But her smiles soon turned to horror as the servant described the bloody scene he had witnessed.

"But where are Karem and Ibi now?" Nitemhe cried, frantically, unable to take it all in. "What has happened to them?"

"I don't know," stammered the terrified servant. "They were still in the temple."

In her anguish, Nitemhe wanted to rush to the temple but the steward, the household's senior servant, managed to hold her back. Calmly, he sent off the servant to fetch Horudj and ushered the distraught Nitemhe inside the house. Then he locked the gates to the courtyard and barricaded the shutters. There was no point in taking any risks. The priests could attack again at any time – the whole family was now in danger.

PART FOUR

Police protection

WHILE THE PRIESTS OF AMUN were brutally attacking his sons, Horudj was in a village on the other side of the river. With business over for the day, he was relaxing with a cup of wine. The servant found him with his friends, enjoying a joke. But the laughter quickly turned to grief as the servant broke the terrible news. At once, Horudj went to the Chief of Police and ordered him to set a watch on his house. The Chief wasted no time. Later, as Nitemhe peeked out of her window, she saw that her house was surrounded by soldiers, armed with shields and spears.

But Horudj did not go back to Teudjoi himself. Perhaps he was frightened for his own life, or perhaps he realised that he had no power over the other priests. Instead, he set off on the six-day journey to Thebes to warn Petiese, and to try to persuade his father-in-law to come back to Teudjoi with him. While she waited for her husband to return, a grief-stricken Nitemhe remained barricaded inside her house, in mourning for her sons. And the soldiers remained on guard. But the police did not try to find the boys' murderers. They were waiting for orders. For only Petiese, the Prophet of Amun, had the power to take action against the guilty priests.

A murder enquiry

WHEN PETIESE FINALLY ARRIVED WITH HORUDJ, the house was still under guard. The Captain of the Royal Bodyguard was sent to meet him and fill him in on the situation. Only then, when Petiese gave them their orders, did the local police set out to arrest the priests who had murdered his grandsons. Horudj tried to comfort his distraught wife. But Nitemhe could not be consoled.

"The boys' bodies are still in the temple," she told him. "Please tell my father to bring them home to me."

On Petiese's orders the police began their search of the temple, but they only found two elderly priests hiding in one of the storerooms. The priests were sent away to Memphis, to be questioned by the Pharaoh. Gradually, though, the police rounded up the remaining priests, including Samut and the High Priests. They were led through the streets of Teudjoi, their hands tied behind their backs. Their future looked bleak. For the Egyptians believed that murder was an offence against the natural order of the universe, and it was punishable by death.

Meanwhile, in the temple, the policemen made a gruesome

find. In a dingy storeroom, crowded with temple jumble and junk, they found the bodies of Horudj's two sons, lying in a corner. It was six days since they had died. At once, Petiese ordered the bodies to be wrapped in linen shrouds and taken back home. It was too much for Nitemhe to bear. As she knelt down to lift the shrouds, she broke down and sobbed as if she would never stop.

Priests on trial

THE TIME FOR JUDGEMENT on the priests of Amun had arrived, and the temple courtyard was now a courtroom. The priests, their wives and children were herded in by the policemen, to await their fate. Petiese stood before them, with Horudj and Nitemhe by his side. Because of his wealth and power, Petiese had been chosen to act as judge at the priests' trial. He had spent years bringing the priesthood under the Pharaoh's control. Now he had it in his power to sentence them all to death. The trial began. The High Priest was the first to plead for his life.

"We know that we have your Honour to thank for making our city and our temple great," he began, solemnly. "The good things that your Honour has done in the name of Amun will remain for ever."

Grim-faced, Petiese stepped forward. He had already decided what he was going to do.

"The good deeds I did were not done for you, but for Amun.

I have a right to see that the priests who murdered my grandsons are brought to justice. But..."

Petiese paused and looked down at his grandsons' killers:

"...with Amun's blessing, I shall let them go."

There was a stunned silence in the courtyard. The astonished priests glanced at each other. None of them could believe what they had heard. One by one, they rose to their feet and looked round at their families, smiling. How the world had changed since Petiese first came to Teudjoi. Then it was in his power to demand whatever punishment he desired but now the Pharaoh had made peace with the priests of Amun. His family had been torn apart but, in the grand scheme of things, his grandsons' murder was no more than a local feud. It could not be allowed to upset the settlement between the Pharaoh and the priests. And, above all else, Petiese was the Pharaoh's man. As always, his duty to his master came first. So it was not forgiveness, but politics, that made him pardon the priests.

Each of the priests stepped forward and bowed before Petiese. When it was Samut's turn, he looked straight into Petiese's eyes with a triumphant look on his face. After all these years of waiting, he had finally had his revenge. On either side of Petiese, Nitemhe and Horudj watched in disbelief as their son's killers filed away. The look of fury on Nitemhe's face said everything – her own father had betrayed her.

Despite his daughter's grief and anger, Petiese had made the right decision. Anything else would have resulted in conflict between priests and pharaoh, and Petiese had worked too hard for too long to allow that to happen.

Family misfortunes

AFTER HIS GRANDSONS' FUNERAL, Petiese prepared to leave Teudjoi once more. His final act was to place an inscription in the temple, to safeguard his family's share of the temple income. But it also carried a warning:

"This man put his heart to set this city in the Pharaoh's service. This tablet records all his good deeds and his priestly offices. He who harms it will lose his sons, his flesh will burn and his name will be lost for eternity."

Just as he was leaving, Nitemhe ran after his chariot. And, just as she had done many years before, she begged him to take her with him.

"Please, take me to Thebes with you," she sobbed. "If I stay here, the priests will kill me."

Petiese leaned forward.

"They cannot," he told his daughter. "As Amun lives, they will never threaten you again."

And then he was gone.

Petiese ended his life in Thebes and died before his master, Pharaoh Psamtek I. His sons continued the family tradition and served the rulers of the new dynasty. We don't know what happened to Nitemhe and Horudj. But, in Teudjoi, the priests of Amun did threaten Petiese's family again. Over the next 150 years, his descendants fought a long battle to keep control of the temple. Petiese's eldest son took over his father's role as Prophet of Amun, but within a generation the priests of Teudjoi had taken back the title, and the family's fifth share of the temple's produce. Despite Petiese's warning, they wiped out all traces of his family by destroying his inscriptions and his statue in the temple. Reduced to poverty, Petiese's great-grandson told the story of his family's downfall in a text known as Rylands Papyrus IX. But the family's fortunes did not improve. By the time Petiese's story was written down, Psamtek's descendants had lost their throne to the Persians. The priests of Amun, however, kept their hold over Egypt's land and wealth for another three hundred years.

CHAPTER FOUR

THE TWINS

Main characters in the story:

Taous (*Tow [how]-us*) and Tages (*Tar-gess*) – *the twins*

Nephoris (*Neff-or-iss*) – *the twins' mother*

Argynoutis (*Ar-gone-oo-tis*) – *the twins' father*

Pakhrates (*Pack-ra-tees*) – *son of Nephoris; the twins' half-brother*

Philippos (*Philip-oss*) – *Nephoris's boyfriend*

Ptolemaios (*Tol-em-eye-oss*) – *temple servant; friend of Argynoutis*

Apollonius (*Apple-own-ee-us*) – *brother of Ptolemaios*

INTRODUCTION

IN THE YEAR 164BC A BLACK AND WHITE BULL, the most sacred animal in Egypt and believed to symbolise the Pharaoh himself, died in the city of Memphis. Crowds of excited onlookers filled the streets to watch the funeral procession pass by on its way to nearby Saqqara where the bull would be buried. There was a festival atmosphere and a growing sense of anticipation as the procession drew near. Around the corner came sixteen priests, carrying the bull's huge, mummified body with its gold death mask. It was a truly spectacular sight. Accompanying the mummy were two young girls, dressed in grey rags, their hair tangled and matted, and their faces covered in ash. They were twins, called Taous and Tages, who had been appointed as the bull's official mourners. It was meant to be a position of honour. But the girls had fallen on very hard times to end up as servants to a dead bull. And they still had further to fall...

Their tragic story survived in a letter which they wrote to the King and Queen of Egypt over two thousand years ago. The letter began:

"To King Ptolemy and Queen Cleopatra,

Greetings from Tages and Taous, twins who perform ritual service in the Great Serapeum at Memphis. Being wronged on many counts by our mother, Nephoris, we flee for refuge to you, that we may obtain justice..."

It went on to tell the story of how two young girls from a good home were left homeless and penniless, and how they struggled to survive in a harsh and money-grabbing world.

PART ONE

Market day

IN THE BUSTLING CLOTH MARKET OF MEMPHIS, it was business as usual. Among the stalls piled high with bolts of brightly coloured fabrics and wool, the stallholders shook out lengths of cloth to show to their customers.

The city of Memphis was home to the twins, Tages and Taous, the daughters of Nephoris and Argynoutis, who were wealthy Egyptian property owners. The twins also had a half-brother, Pakhrates, from their mother's first marriage. Today, they were accompanying their mother to market to sell some of their home-produced linen cloth. Snootily, Nephoris walked slowly past the stalls, checking on the quality of the cloth. At one stall, she stopped and pushed the twins forward with their bundles of cloth. The stallholder unfolded a length of the cloth and held it up to the light. Then he offered Nephoris a price.

"Are you mad?" she exclaimed. "This is the finest linen you're ever likely to see. What you're offering is daylight robbery."

And she made as if to walk off with the twins.

It worked. The stallholder upped his price; Nephoris upped hers. Eventually, they struck a deal and the stallholder counted some coins into Nephoris's hand. As she turned to go, she spotted a handsome Greek soldier smiling at her from the doorway. Then he walked away. Pretending not to notice, Nephoris turned to the twins:

"You two can go home now," she said. "I've got some other business to see to here."

Once they'd gone, Nephoris walked quickly out of the market, in the same direction as the soldier.

Secrets and scandals

THE SOLDIER'S NAME WAS PHILIPPOS and he was no stranger to Nephoris. In fact, they were having an affair. But Nephoris was angry with him for turning up at the market. If the twins had seen him, their secret would have been out. In ancient Egypt, adultery was a serious crime. If Nephoris's husband, Argynoutis, found out she had been unfaithful, she risked losing everything – her money, her property and her reputation. And she was not about to let that happen. Cunning Nephoris had a plan that would allow her to keep it all – and Philippos, too. Making sure that no one was watching them, she began to whisper into Philippos's ear...

When Nephoris returned home later that afternoon, Argynoutis was sitting outside in the courtyard, drinking wine with a friend. She smiled at him as she went inside. If she wanted

RULES OF THE PTOLEMIES

In 332BC, Alexander the Great of Macedonia arrived in Egypt. He was greeted as a hero because he had conquered the tyrannical Persians who ruled Egypt. Alexander was careful to respect Egyptian culture and religion, and founded a great new city, called Alexandria, on the Mediterranean coast. When Alexander died in 323BC, his vast empire was divided up. His Greek general, Ptolemy, took control of Egypt and, in 305BC, declared himself Pharaoh and founded a new dynasty, which was to rule Egypt for the next 250 years. At the time of the twins' story, in 164BC, Ptolemy VI and his sister, Cleopatra II, ruled Egypt.

to, there were magic spells to get rid of unwanted husbands...

"Take a mouse and drown it in some water, then make the man drink it. It will make him blind in both eyes. Grind its body up with food, and make him eat it. He will swell up and die."

But Nephoris didn't believe in magic. It was much too risky. She had a much better idea up her sleeve. When Argynoutis said goodnight to his friend and came into the house, Philippos slipped silently into the courtyard and hid by the doorway to the living room. Unfortunately, as he moved backwards, he knocked over a water jar. When Argynoutis went to investigate, Philippos quickly drew his sword and lunged at him, catching him on the shoulder. There was chaos as Argynoutis tried to duck out of the way. But worse was to come. When Argynoutis ran back to the living room and tried to get into his house, and safety, he could not open the door. Nephoris had slammed it shut and locked it. Desperate now, Argynoutis ran into the street, closely followed by Philippos. Panting heavily, Argynoutis ran down a street towards the Nile. But when he rounded the corner, he found himself... at a dead end. He turned, to see Philippos smiling triumphantly. Argynoutis knew that he was trapped. He looked at Philippos, then at the river. Then he jumped in.

Falling on hard times

EARLY NEXT MORNING, Nephoris stood and watched as Philippos pushed Tages and Taous through the door of their father's house and threw them out on to the street.

"Now get lost," she said, throwing a bundle of clothes after them. "And don't bother coming back."

For Nephoris, the twins were a problem. They were old enough to get married, but marriage would mean giving them a dowry of a third of the family property. A rich Egyptian widow was a good catch for a Greek soldier like Philippos. An Egyptian widow with two daughters was much less so. Taous screamed as the door was slammed shut behind them, then began to cry. What would become of them now? With no family to look after them and only a few silver coins between them, they would soon be starving. As the daughters of a wealthy family, both of the girls were well educated. But being able to read and write would not help them find work for themselves. Jobs as scribes and officials were only open to men.

Dejectedly, the twins slumped down on a brick bench in the street and wondered what to do next. Neither of them could think of anything. Just then a man walked by, leading a camel. And it gave Tages an idea…

"Where are you going?" she asked the man.

"To Saqqara," he replied.

"Can you give us a lift?" asked Tages. "We can pay you in silver."

And she handed over one of their precious coins.

"Climb on board," said the camel driver.

The girls hitched up their skirts and climbed on to the camel. Then the man led them off down the street. The temple town of Saqqara, on the edge of the desert, lay a few kilometres to the west of Memphis. It was famous as a place of shelter for those who had fallen on hard times. It was also a place where ordinary people like the twins could get their story heard. Besides, Tages had remembered that Saqqara was the home of a friend of their father's, called Ptolemaios. Perhaps he would take them in and help them to win back their inheritance. If not, they were in deep trouble.

Family life was important to the ancient Egyptians, but when things went wrong, as it had for the twins, the future could be bleak indeed. Friendless, homeless and almost penniless, they faced a life fraught with danger on the streets unless their father's old friend was able to help them

95

PART TWO

Dreams and pilgrims

IT WAS EARLY MORNING IN SAQQARA, the city of dreams. In the Temple of Astarte, Ptolemaios walked along a corridor lined with open doorways. As he passed each door, he glanced quickly inside. In each of the small chambers, lit by a window, a person lay sleeping on a reed mat. These rooms were the dream chambers. Each year, thousands of pilgrims flocked to the temples at Saqqara, where the highlight of their visit was to spend a night in a dream chamber. The Egyptians believed that dreams were messages from the gods. Here they hoped that the gods would help to solve their problems, cure their aches and pains, or predict the future. In the morning, they told their dreams to Ptolemaios, who interpreted their meaning by consulting his book of dreams.

In one of the chambers, a pilgrim was just waking up. Ptolemaios sat down beside him and began to take notes.

"A dove flew out of my hand," the pilgrim began, "and I ran after it. I wasn't going to let it escape. I caught it again and held on to it tightly..."

Just then, Ptolemaios's younger brother, Apollonius, came into the room and whispered a few words in his ear. Ptolemaios looked puzzled. He apologised to the pilgrim, then followed Apollonius out of the temple and into a busy street. This was the Dromos, a wide, paved street, lined with stalls, temples and shrines that ran through the centre of the Serapeum, the walled sanctuary

THE MEANING OF DREAMS

The ancient Egyptians believed gods communicated with them through dreams, which they called 'revelations of Truth'. Dreams could predict the future or give advice. Pharaohs often claimed that a god had appeared to them in a dream to instruct them to wage war or to warn them of danger. People spent the night in a temple dream chamber so the god could speak directly to them. Their dreams were interpreted by trained priests and temple servants. They had dream books to help them, which listed various dreams and their meanings. Dreaming of a large cat meant good fortune. Other common dreams included breaking stones, losing teeth, a shining moon, and drowning in the River Nile.

that had been Ptolemaios's home for eight years. Inside were shops, lodgings, houses and shrines to many of the gods, including the burial place of Egypt's most sacred animal, the Apis bull.

Ptolemaios lived and worked in the temple of the goddess Astarte, inside the Serapeum. A sign outside the temple advertised his dream business. Eight years ago, Ptolemaios had signed a contract with the temple. In return for his job as an interpreter of dreams, he took a religious vow never to leave the walls of the Serapeum again. His younger brother, Apollonius, was his main contact with the outside world. Now Apollonius led him to the twins, who were watching the pilgrims buying trinkets and keepsakes of their visit from the souvenir stalls. Tages stepped forward and introduced herself.

"We're Tages and Taous," she explained. "We're the daughters of Argynoutis."

Then she burst into tears.

Despite his surprise, Ptolemaios greeted them warmly.

"Don't cry, my dear," he said, kindly. "Come home with me and tell me everything that's happened."

Ptolemaios's room was small and simply furnished, with a bare earth floor. The girls sat on a reed mat in the corner, while he fetched some bread and water. Then he settled down to listen to their story. Tages did most of the talking...

"... Philippos wounded our father and we haven't seen him again... Then our mother threw us out... And now we don't have any money or a home, or anything..."

Ptolemaios listened in horror, and shook his head in disbelief at the way they had been treated. He was a temple servant, not a priest, and not a rich man. But for his old friend's sake, he agreed to take the twins in.

Pleading their case

A KILOMETRE OR SO FROM THE SERAPEUM stood the Anubieion, the great temple enclosure dedicated to Anubis, the jackal-headed god of embalming. Apollonius led the girls inside. The Anubieion provided lodgings for pilgrims, many of whom were milling around. But it was also the place where the ordinary citizens of Memphis could go for legal advice. The twins followed Apollonius into the office of the notary, the official whose job was to solve any legal wrangles over business and property. If anyone could help the twins, it was the notary.

In the office, Tages and Taous sat down on stools and nervously waited to plead their case. When their turn came, the notary listened carefully to their story and made a few notes. Then he walked over to a shelf and took down a book of legal cases, which he leafed through. Scratching his forehead thoughtfully, he looked at the anxious girls.

"I'm sorry," he said, patting them on the heads. "But there's nothing I can do."

While their father's fate was still unknown, the twins had no rights to their inheritance. They had no idea that their father was already dead. Back in Memphis, in the courtyard of Nephoris's house, two men laid a body, wrapped in matting, on the ground. Unmoved, Nephoris and Philippos looked on. It was Argynoutis. He had been rescued from the river and taken to his brother's house. But he died shortly afterwards and his brother brought his body home to be buried. Next day, acting the part of a grief-stricken widow, Nephoris took her dead husband's belongings to market to sell. According to custom, this money would pay for his burial. But Nephoris had no intention of burying her husband, and making sure he enjoyed a comfortable afterlife. While she was gone, Philippos and Pakhrates threw the shrouded body into a donkey cart and drove off into the desert. For the way to get rid of an unwanted corpse was to leave it unburied in the desert.

In Ptolemaios's little room, Tages and Taous hugged each other and sobbed. We don't know how the tragic news reached the twins in Saqqara. But we do know that they firmly believed their father had died of despair. Now they had no money, no family, no home and no prospects. And kind though Ptolemaios was, his meagre income would not support all three of them for very much longer.

PART THREE

Death of a bull

ONE DAY, an excited Apollonius came running into the dream chambers, searching for Ptolemaios.

"The bull is dead!" he shouted. "The bull is dead!"

It was 7 April 164BC, and news of another death had arrived from Memphis. But this time, it was good news. The Apis bull, the most sacred animal in Egypt, had died in his temple. The brothers and stall-keepers ran out into the street, followed by the pilgrims. The death of the bull was a national event, as important as the death of a Pharaoh. It was an event that the people of the Serapeum had been waiting fourteen years for. Now there would be a great festival as the sacred animal was brought to the Serapeum to be buried, amid great pomp and ceremony. For Ptolemaios, it was especially thrilling. He had been confined inside the walls of the Serapeum for years. Now the world would come to him. And in this festival of mourning,

TEMPLE TOWN

Saqqara, where the twins' story unfolds, was a major religious centre near Memphis. Pilgrims flocked here from all over Egypt to visit the temples and dream chambers. The town was divided into a number of temple enclosures, which were like mini cities, with temples, shrines, food and souvenir stalls, guesthouses and lodgings. They included the Serapeum, where Ptolemaios and the twins lived. The Serapeum contained the vast catacombs of the dead Apis bulls. The bull's temple was Saqqara's greatest tourist attraction. A long road called the Dromos, lined with statues of sphinxes, linked the two main enclosures, the Serapeum and the Anubieion.

he hoped to find a special role for the twins that would turn their fortunes around.

A shaven-headed priest made his way to the front of a nearby temple to make an announcement. Immediately, a chattering crowd gathered in front of him. Hearing the commotion, the twins ran out of the Temple of Astarte to find Ptolemaios and see what all the fuss what about.

"Come here! Come here!" shouted Ptolemaios, taking their hands. "Get to the front of the crowd. Quick. I've got an idea."

Custom said that, when the Apis bull died, a pair of female twins was appointed to take on the roles of the goddesses, Isis and Nephthys, the chief mourners of the dead bull. Twins were rare in the ancient world and, in Egypt, they were treated as special. But this time, the temple did not have far to look for its sacred twins. Clued-up Ptolemaios saw his chance and grabbed it. Before the startled girls could speak, he pushed them to the front of the crowd, and presented them to the priest.

Later that day, the twins once again found themselves sitting in the notary's office in the Anubieion. The notary looked at them carefully, then wrote out a contract on a sheet of papyrus. Being chosen to serve the Apis bull was a great honour. Better still, it guaranteed the twins an income for life,

SACRED ANIMALS

Many Egyptian gods and goddesses were linked to birds and animals. These creatures were often kept in the deity's cult (main) temple where, it was believed, the deity's spirit passed into them. The most sacred animal in Egypt was the Apis bull. It was associated with the god Ptah, whose main temple was in Memphis, and also symbolised the Pharaoh's power. When a bull died, a search was made all over Egypt for its successor. The new bull had to be black and white, with a white, triangular patch on his forehead. Then he and his mother were taken to Memphis where they lived in great comfort for the rest of their lives paid from the temple funds. The notary handed them some wooden ration tokens. Their contract also gave them a special bonus ration of castor oil during the seventy days of mourning. It wouldn't replace the inheritance their mother had cheated them of, but they could trade the oil for a good price and save some money for the future. The notary signed his name at the bottom of the contract, and gave it to Tages for safekeeping.

But the twins' new position had a double edge. Soon a new bull would be found and installed in his temple in Memphis. But the twins were the servants of the dead bull in Saqqara and were forbidden to marry until the new bull died. A bull could live for twenty-five years or more. If the twins were unlucky, they would be forty years old by the time they could leave the bull's service. Certainly, they would have some money, but they would also be well beyond marriageable age.

In mourning

BACK IN PTOLEMAIOS'S ROOM, the twins busily daubed each others' faces with ash. Ash-covered faces, smudged black eye-liner to look like tears, tangled hair and grey cloaks were the mourning clothes of ancient Egypt. For the next seventy days, until the bull was buried in Saqqara, the twins would walk to Memphis every day and lead the crowds of visitors mourning the bull in its temple.

At this time, records show, Ptolemaios wrote down a dream

which Tages had. Despite everything that had happened, she still dreamed of being reunited with her mother. She told Ptolemaios what she had dreamt...

"I dreamt I was in Memphis. The river had flooded and the water was high. I saw my mother standing on the opposite bank. So I took off my clothes and swam across the river to her. She said, 'You are welcome,' and took me back home with her."

But the thought of their mother ever welcoming them back home was just that – a dream.

In Memphis, the priests were preparing to mummify the Apis bull. The embalming tent was inside one of the temple chambers, where the body of a huge black and white bull lay on an alabaster table. A priest ushered the twins into the temple and towards the shrine, where a statue of the Apis bull stood, garlanded with flowers and dressed in an embroidered linen shroud. A group of six women followed them inside. These were the professional mourners who dropped to their knees in front of the statue and started to sway back and forth, their hands held high above their heads. Hesitantly, Tages and Taous knelt down and copied them. As a crowd of curious pilgrims looked on, they joined in with the mourners, pulling their hair and wailing. Taous badly wanted to giggle, until her sister shot her a dagger-like look.

Unseen by the twins, Nephoris and two of her friends were in the crowd. Surprised, one of the women spotted the twins and pointed them out to their mother as they walked into the temple with the priests. No wonder Nephoris looked astonished to see her daughters in their starring role.

A mother's scheming

BACK HOME, NEPHORIS TOLD PHILIPPOS what she had seen. She had already sold half of her husband's property and invested the proceeds in land and property which were in her own name. Her daughters would never see the third of their father's money which was due to them. And now scheming Nephoris had worked out a way of profiting from the twins' good fortune. She called for Pakhrates, her son, and told him her treacherous plan.

Next day, as the exhausted twins walked down the street in Memphis on their way home from performing their duties, their mother's two friends caught up with them and greeted them warmly. The twins exchanged anxious glances. What did the women want? Were they genuinely pleased to see them? Or did they have other things in mind? Taous wanted to ignore them and carried on walking. But curious Tages pulled her back. Then one of the women turned round and called, "Pakhrates!" For this was when the twins' half-brother appeared in their lives again.

Hearing the woman's call, a sheepish-looking Pakhrates appeared from a side street. He walked over to the girls, who eyed him suspiciously. Then, putting his hand on his heart, Pakhrates dropped to his knees and apologised for letting his mother treat them so badly and begged their forgiveness. It was a horribly convincing display. So convincing that Tages stepped forward, took his hands and gently helped him to his feet. Taous was more reluctant but eventually she came and stood next to her sister. A delighted Pakhrates hugged his half-sisters. We do not know why the twins decided to trust Pakhrates again. Perhaps he told them that he too had been thrown out of the house? Or perhaps they thought meeting him would lead to a longed-for reunion with their mother? Whatever the reason, the twins offered to take their half-brother back to their sanctuary in the Serapeum.

PART FOUR

A funeral procession

AS THE DAY OF THE BULL'S BURIAL APPROACHED, the town of Saqqara filled with pilgrims. Crowds of visitors milled around the Dromos, browsing among the souvenir stalls and haggling over the price of goods. Money was changing hands at an amazing rate and the stall-keepers were doing a roaring trade. Two special temple policemen were on duty to keep the crowd in order. Despite the solemn occasion, there was a festival atmosphere in the town, for today they would celebrate the bull's rebirth as a god. This was a massive event in Saqqara's history, when people from all over Egypt flocked to the town.

Meanwhile, in Ptolemaios's room, Tages pulled her money pouch from a pot and gave Pakhrates some coins. Then she put it back in its hiding place. But not before Pakhrates had caught a glimpse of the coins, ration tokens and the sheet of papyrus inside. Then, dressed in their mourning clothes, the twins left for Memphis. While they performed their duties, their half-brother stayed behind and took charge of the household chores.

This was an important day for the twins. Today, the mummified bull began its journey from Memphis to its final resting place in the Serapeum. A hush fell over the crowd waiting outside the bull's temple in Memphis. Then they let out a loud shriek of lamentation as a priest stepped out of the temple and held up a piece of cloth which he tore in two. This was the sign they had been waiting for. From inside the temple compound appeared the enormous, mummified bull, wearing a gold death mask and sitting on a sledge, held up by priests. As the priests passed the twins, they lowered the sledge so the girls could take their place on either side of the bull. Then it was raised on to the priests' shoulders, with the twins on board. Four priests, carrying banners showing images of the gods, walked in front, while a row of professional mourners followed behind. The sweet smell of incense filled the air and the sound of wailing mixed with the beating of drums and the chanting of the crowd. People gasped as the fabulous funeral procession passed through the streets – it was a truly spectacular sight.

A burial and a theft

CAREFUL NOT TO BE SPOTTED BY THE TWINS, Pakhrates slinked up to his mother and Philippos standing among the crowd. He whispered something to them, then ran back to

Saqqara, along the deserted Dromos. In the dream chambers, Pakhrates crept silently along the passage towards the twins' room. His heart missed a beat as he heard a noise, and pressed himself against the wall. But it was only Ptolemaios leaving to join the procession, and he was too busy with his own thoughts to notice an intruder.

It was a proud day for Ptolemaios. With Apollonius next to him, he stood on the steps of the Temple of Astarte to watch the procession arrive. As the twins passed by, he caught their eyes and waved delightedly. Then he and his brother fell in behind the mourners as they went through the temple gateway.

MUMMIFICATION

When the bull died, its body was mummified so that its soul would survive in the next world. First it was taken to the tent of purification, for washing and anointing with oils. In the embalming tent, its throat was cut to drain its blood, and its organs were removed. These were mummified separately and placed in containers called canopic jars. Natron salt was packed around the body to dry it out, then it was stuffed with bags of sawdust and salt. When it was dry, it was wrapped in bandages, with jewellery and charms between the layers. A gold death mask was placed on its head, inlaid with precious stones for eyes. Then the mummified bull was taken in a great procession to Saqqara, to be placed in its coffin and buried in the catacombs.

The final resting place for the bull was in the catacombs beneath the Serapeum, where it joined the bodies of previous bulls and took its place among the gods. As the procession approached the ramp leading down into the catacombs, the sledge was lowered to the ground and the twins got off. In front of the bull, two dancers performed a ritual dance which symbolised the step over the threshold between this life and the next. Once the bull was buried, the catacombs would be sealed until the next bull died. And, until that day came, Tages and Taous would be the bull's servants.

As the mummified bull was being lowered into its vast black stone coffin, the twins' half-brother, Pakhrates, sneaked into Ptolemaios's room and stole the twins' money and ration tokens.

Fight for justice

THAT NIGHT, THE TWINS RETURNED TO THEIR ROOM, exhausted from their day's duties. Taous flopped down on her mat and fell asleep almost at once. Tages called to Pakhrates, but there was no reply. She ran into the next room, but her half-brother was nowhere to be seen. Then a terrible thought struck her. She grabbed the pot where their tokens and money were hidden, and turned it upside down. To her horror, it was empty.

"Pakhrates has stolen our money!" she cried, shaking her sister awake. "Now what are we going to do?"

Once again, their mother had taken everything they owned.

Meanwhile, in their father's house in Memphis, Nephoris looked on greedily as Pakhrates emptied a handful of coins and some wooden ration tokens on to the table. Then he took out the sheet of papyrus on which the twins' special rations of castor oil were reckoned up. Pakhrates started to read it out to his mother but she snatched it out of his hands.

And this is how Tages and Taous came to send a letter pleading their case to King Ptolemy. In fact, Ptolemaios wrote it down for them as they dictated it. The letter began:

"To King Ptolemy and Queen Cleopatra,

Greetings from Tages and Taous, twins who perform ritual service in the Great Serapeum in Memphis... We beg you to send our petition to the local officials so that they do not pay our mother either the oil that belongs to us or anything else of ours. Compel her also to return whatever of our father's she holds illegally so that we are helped through you. May you prosper."

Sadly, in spite of their service to the Apis bull, the twins' letter fell on deaf ears. Tages and Taous never got their inheritance back, nor their stolen money or rations. We don't know how long they had to wait to be released from their duties to the dead bull. But we do know that Ptolemaios lived on in the Serapeum, interpreting pilgrims' dreams. He had no hope of ever being set free from his temple service, and his letters show him becoming more and more fed up with life in Saqqara. But his precious collection of letters and dreams has survived to this day, and gives us a unique picture of life in the temple town. And one hundred and fifty years after this story, the last

Pharaoh, Cleopatra, died, and Egypt became another part of the ever-expanding Roman Empire. The cult of the Apis bull lived on for another four centuries until the Roman Emperor ordered the Serapeum to be destroyed. And with this, three thousand years of Egyptian religion came to an end.